THE UNUSUAL MEXICAN:

A STUDY

IN

ACCULTURATION

RUTH L. MARTINEZ

THE UNUSUAL MEXICAN
A STUDY IN ACCULTURATION

by

Ruth Lucretia Martinez

A Thesis

Claremont Colleges

1942

Reprinted in 1973 by
R AND E RESEARCH ASSOCIATES
4843 Mission Street, San Francisco 94112
18581 McFarland Avenue, Saratoga, California 95070

Publishers and Distributors of Ethnic Studies
Editor: Adam S. Eterovich
Publisher: Robert D. Reed

Library of Congress Card Catalog Number
70-167580

ISBN
0-88247-214-3

PREFACE

To the young men and women, their parents and families, through whose kindliness and generosity the material for this study has been made available, grateful acknowledgment is made. Without the helpful suggestions and criticisms of the groups concerned with the problems of the Mexican in this country, particularly Los Colegentes Mexicanos and the Mexican Youth Conference, much of the material included would lose its touch with conditions as they exist today.

To Mr. Cecil L. Dunn and the other members of the Faculty of Claremont who have given of their time beyond the limits of necessity, deep thanks is rendered.

To the Mexican people who have been grateful for the interest of an American in their adjustment, let it be said that their contribution to the common fruition of our cultures ensures the happiness of the future.

Let not ambition mock their useful toil,
 Their homely joys, and destiny obscure;
Nor grandeur hear with a disdainful smile
 The short and simple annals of the poor.

                                    Thomas Gray

Elegy Written in a Country Church Yard, 1751

CONTENTS

INTRODUCTION

With the world as we have known it disintegrating before our eyes, and life as we have lived it turned into an enormous question mark, the adaptability of an individual group seems rather insignificant. However, with the modern psychological and educational system geared to the theory of the worth of the individual, a group of the size and quality of the unusual[1] Mexican girl and boy has a significance to the readjustment of our way of life.

This study proposes to examine the processes whereby the acculturation of the Mexican group has been effected in schools, community life, and social relationships. The study further intends to note the influence of each of these in the acceleration of his adjustment to the American group. Since the study must be held in bounds, the Unusual Mexican, as defined, has been selected as the group to be considered.

Eduard Lindeman in his Social Discovery suggests the role of a "participant observer."[2] This method requires observers who have a vital interest in the group under observation and who watch its behavior from the viewpoint of a sharer.[3] The participant in group activity may see things which the outside observer could never see, but his sharing must be kept in mind as it is an influence on the group. This fact must be realized and its effect on the situation taken into consideration, so that proper allowance may be made for it.

In the study of social processes it is necessary to secure an accurate account of what occurs in the group. The material obtained should be so objective that any other observer could duplicate it. This indicates that the data must be obtained with a minimum of questions that would call for rationalization.

---

[1]An unusual Mexican is defined, for the purpose of this thesis, as one who has graduated from the Chaffey High School or Junior College since June 1932, and including June 1941. (See Appendix.)

[2]Eduard C. Lindeman, Social Discovery (New York: Longmans-Green, 1925), p. 191.

[3]The writer has taught the Mexicans in the Chaffey district for over twelve years, and knows many of the groups under discussion. It is therefore obvious that the opinions expressed are colored by these friendships.

Many methods have been used in this study to obtain the necessary material, but special attention has been given to the life history, since it reveals how the habits of the past have been preserved, what effect the conflict of cultures has upon the Mexican,[4] and how he is adjusting to the new life into which he has been thrust. With this purpose in mind it becomes necessary to define the problem.

---

[4]"Mexican" is used to denote people of Mexican parentage. "American" denotes the people native to the United States. This is the distinction made by Emory S. Bogardus in The Mexican in the United States (Los Angeles: University of Southern California Press, 1934), p. 9.

CHAPTER I

THE COMMUNITY, THE PEOPLE, AND THEIR PROBLEM

The Mexican under consideration is "unusual" in one aspect. He has completed either High School, or Junior College, or both. This standard of "unusualness" has been arbitrarily set, since there was no existing ruler for measuring Mexican patterns of performance. The purpose of the study, in general, is to attempt to analyze the process by which the unusual Mexican has attained that status. The reasons underlying his ability to complete a high school or junior college education, while so many of his race drop out from the 5th grade up through the early high school years, must constitute a commentary on either the social and educational factors in the United States, or upon the ability of the Mexican to adapt himself to our systems.

The scope of the problem, self-evidently, is enormous, and for that reason has been limited to the physical boundaries of a small district, in order that the personal data called for by the type of study might be more readily obtained. The Chaffey School District of San Bernardino County, California, was set arbitrarily as the district to be considered since it is a section with which the observer is familiar and which contains several large permanent Mexican colonies. It is a district composed of ten smaller grammar school districts stretched out over 222 square miles, containing three sizable towns and six villages, drawing from a population of approximately 41,382.[1] It produces mainly citrus crops, grapes and grape products, some deciduous fruits, and has in its environs some fair sized and many small manufacturing units. These industries have been the reason for Mexican migration to this district. The year-round picking seasons for the crops of the district have served to increase the number of permanently settled Mexicans living in the Chaffey District.

The pattern of the economic activity of the community explains, in part, the extent of the employment of Mexicans, and the varying duration of the employment of a single person. The orange crop is harvested throughout the year, beginning with Navels from January to June, and the Valencias from July through November.

---

[1]U.S. Census, 1940.

1

Only December and June are slack months, and of course on rainy days work is stopped. The lemon crop is year long also, with an accent on the summer months while the demand is high, slacking off during the winter months. Grapes are picked and crushed from August through November, while pruning begins in December, and ground aerating is done in the spring months. Deciduous crops begin about the 15th of June and rotate in kinds until the 15th of October, with the drying yards at full time from the end of June until the end of July. Pruning begins in January and lasts through March. The manufacturers, for the main part, provide year-round jobs, with occasional slack seasons, depending on the nature of the product. Although weather affects the number of days worked, and the slack seasons are inevitable, sufficient work is provided, by rotating labor with the crops, to keep the average Mexican family from want. Each family must keep in hand a contact with the next fruit crop, so that as the new season begins it may be assured of a job, thus creating almost continuous employment.

Table I

CROP AND JOB ROTATION

Jan. Feb. Mar. Apr. May June July Aug. Sept. Oct. Nov. Dec.

Oranges:
  Navels
  Valencias

Lemons

Grapes

Deciduous

---------- light season
_____ heavy season

The tremendous influx of Mexican workers brought to work the crops began soon after 1910. The gates were let down at the American borders. Train loads rolled across the lines. They came in carts and cars, by bus, on foot, in literal droves, lured by the big American dollar. The following is a table of immigration taken from the Report of the Commissioner General of Immigration, Washington, D.C., from 1900 to 1933.[2]

Year	Number	Percent of Total Immigration
1900-1910	49,642	0.6
1911	19,889	2.3
1912	23,238	2.8
1913	11,926	1.0
1914	14,614	1.2
1915	12,340	3.8
1916	18,425	6.2
1917	17,869	6.0
1918	18,524	16.8
1919	29,818	21.1
1920	52,361	12.2
1921	30,758	3.8
1922	19,551	6.3
1923	63,768	12.2
1924	89,336	12.6
1925	32,964	11.2
1926	43,316	14.2
1927	57,721	20.2
1928	59,016	19.2
1929	40,154	14.3
1930	11,915	5.2
1931	2,627	3.4
1932	1,674	1.7
1933	1,514	0.6

After the debacle of October 1929, this large group of workers was left in a pitable state. Relief loads were increased past the point of handling by the then existing agencies. The social services were inundated. Many Mexican families who so desired were sent back to Mexico.[3] Those Mexicans who remained are considered to be our permanent Mexican population. Immigration has almost ceased in comparison to the "highs" reached during the 1920's. Those persons immigrating prior to and during that time are the parents of the young people under discussion.

_____

[2]Emory S. Bogardus, The Mexican in the United States (Los Angeles: The University of Southern California, 1934), p. 14.

[3]Ibid., p. 15.

The broad back and strong muscles of the Mexican laborer, his ability to work in a hot, dry climate, his genial and docile acceptance of life as it comes, were the "open sesame" to his labors in America. From this group, alike in racial strain and cultural background, came the girls and boys born in Mexico or the United States who have been among the graduates from Chaffey High School or Junior College during the past ten years.

Because of the nature of the world in this period, the financial stress, the increase of government participation in social welfare, and the rise of experimentation in forms of government, these years constitute a period of noteworthy change. The group under discussion is a significant cross section of Mexicans in a difficult time. The incidence of acculturation in times as stirring as the years from 1932 to 1941 gives some evidence of the natural adaptability of the Mexican under pressure. For this reason, and the obvious necessity for limiting the number of Mexican girls and boys to be considered, the period from June 1932 to June 1941, containing ten graduating classes in both the High School and Junior College has been chosen for use in obtaining names and data for the study of "Unusual Mexican" young people.

It is obvious to anyone who is a resident of Southern California, a section which contains more Mexicans than any other division in the United States,[4] that the Mexican is a problem of some importance.

During the period of the Madera, Carranza, and Huerta revolutions that extended from 1910 through the 1920's, the sociological and historical writers, each with his own theme to plug, kept the presses rolling. During the upheavals of the next twenty years, which covered the controversial regimes of Calles, Obregon, and Cardenas, the land reforms, the church curtailment, and the educational renaissance, did not lend themselves to calm discourse and unheated consideration. So the Mexican, both at home and in this strange America, became a person of mystery, unknown ability, and suspected design. The general consensus was that "he has muscles of steel, and we have acted as though we thought he had just about sense enough to use them with the pick and shovel. He has been a good man to dig our ditches, to

---

[4]Jovita Gonzalez de Mireles, "Latin America" in Our Racial and National Minorities, edited by Francis J. Brown and Joseph Rouck (New York: Prentice-Hall, Inc., 1939), p. 502.

4

tamp our railroad ties, to pick our oranges, our cotton, our fruit, and, in fact, to do all of the manual labor which we consider ourselves too good to do. But from the neck up we have not had a very good opinion of our neighbor Juan."[5]

Leading authorities themselves vary in their opinion of the mental ability of the mental ability of the Mexican. Manuel Gamio, an outstanding anthropologist and leader of the educational movement in Mexico, believes that the Mexican in the United States is given very unfair mental tests, for two important reasons: (1) because of his language handicap, and (2) because of the differences in the experiences of the Mexican child, the difference being in the relatively scientific atmosphere in which the American child is raised as compared with the supernatural, magical, folklore background of the average Mexican home. He says: "The mental capacity of the Mexican child is probably normal, although some investigators conclude that he is mentally inferior to the American child of the same age--a conclusion probably affected by racial attitudes and by a translation into terms of mental competence of differences in economic and cultural position."[6]

Dr. Goodwin B. Watson, in a letter to Bruno Lasker, suggests that in testing children, when proper corrections for language and subject matter have been made, differences between races are smaller than at first appear. He says that "it seems probable that American Indians and Mexicans show even less than the Negro on the average, of the sort of ability measured by intelligence tests. The fact of major importance, however, is that the difference within each of these racial groups are very much larger than the differences in the averages. A child of any race may be bright or dull."[7]

Emory S. Bogardus makes the following statements:

"About one half of the cases handled by a given probation officer
for Mexican boys are border-line or mentally defective. There
I.Q.s range around 70. Only one in a group of 125 had an I.Q.
over 105. The border line for Mexican children is about 10 points

---

[5]Robert N. McLean, That Mexican (New York: Fleming H. Revell Company, 1928), p. 26.

[6]Manuel Gamio, Mexican Immigration to the United States (Chicago: University of Chicago Press, 1930), pp. 72-73.

[7]Bruno Lasker, Race Attitudes in Children (New York: Henry Holt and Company, 1929), p. 90.

below that for other children in the United States, because of language difficulty. ...[8]

"At the time he enrolls in school, his one bright hope is the sympathetic American teacher. Under her tutelage he makes a creditable showing. During his first years of schooling he does as well as American children in penmanship, and about as well in manual work, three fourths as well in vocabulary, arithmetic, and memorization tests. His language handicap, his inferior habits of living, the uncertain labor conditions which affect his parents, generally explain his tendency to fall behind, to grow discouraged and to drop out of school in his early teens. Whether the intelligence tests do him justice or not may be a disputed question, but the results indicate that, on the whole, he falls below American children in intelligence."[9]

In a thesis on "The Comparative Intelligence of the Mexican Child," Rollin Drake summarizes the findings of multiple intelligence and achievement tests given both American and Mexican children in San Antonio, Texas. He says that "as a group, when considered from the standpoint of both intelligence and achievement, the mean of the Mexican children is lower than that for the white children by an amount which is equal to about half of the spread of the middle two thirds of either group." He finds, from his observations, that the language handicap is of little importance by the time the Mexican child has reached the sixth grade, and that the over-ageness from this language handicap, coupled with the earlier maturation age of the Mexican, is the real problem of the Mexican in the upper grades.[10]

Most Mexican children in the American schools are over age, that is, past the average age for their grades. Almost all Mexican children are required to spend at least one year in a pre-primary grade, in which the emphasis is placed on learning English. This retardation, in part, ex plains the over-ageness.

The language handicap, undoubtedly, is a major one for the Mexican. In a San Bernardino County study, made by Merton E. Hill, it was found that 78.5 percent of the Mexican children were over age, as against 33.3 percent of the American children enrolled; that the Mexican student averaged four years behind the American child in

---

[8]Op. cit., p. 56.

[9]Ibid., p. 68.

[10]Rollin Drake, "The Comparative Intelligence of the Mexican Child," (unpublished Master's Thesis, The University of Southern California, Los Angeles, 1938), p. 74.

6

grade placement, although the definite conclusion that the language handicap alone accounted for this could not be reached.[11] It would seem that the addition of environmental disadvantages to the language drawback would provide an adequate explanation for many of the failures charged up to the Mexican child.

But above this average group of Mexican children rise here and there girls and boys of exceptional ability. Not all of the outstanding Mexican young people are included in this study, since many of them failed to accomplish four years of high school during the 1930's, a task which required, in addition to ability, financial backing, family participation, and ambition. The combination of reasons for the "staying power" of the Mexican boy and girl will be one of the valuable data to be gained from this study.

The place of accommodation in the struggle to Americanize and assimilate the Mexican cannot be too highly emphasized.[12] The degree to which the unusual Mexican has to become Americanized--that is, to have acquired the so-called American culture, in comparison with other Mexicans without his accomplishments--will be another valuable commentary on his ability. It has been pointed out that "Americanizing the American"[13] is often a harder task, when it includes the lofty ideals of neighborliness, tolerance and cooperation, than to build on to the already high social-consciousness of the Mexican.

From the purely selfish standpoint of the teacher of Mexican children, the results of years of work are almost heartbreaking. Only an occasional bright spot, the once-in-a-while, of an unusual Mexican, serves to cheer her on. Are the labors

---

[11]Merton E. Hill, "The Development of an Americanization Program at Chaffey Junior College" (unpublished Master's Thesis, The University of Southern California, Los Angeles, 1928), p. 28.

[12]It is an interesting fact that for some time the Mexican government has had a "Mexicanization" program carried on throughout its Federal Rural Schools. The problem of assimilating the thirty Indian tribes and languages, as well as preserving native arts and music, is a vital part of the new concept of Dr. Moizes Saenz, Minister of Education.

William E. Walling, The Mexican Question (New York: Robins Press, 1927), p. 69.

[13]Stella E. Hanson, "Mexican Laborers in the Southwest" (unpublished Master's Thesis, Pomona College, Claremont, 1926), p. 27.

of these thousands of teachers wasted? Is the educative process with Mexicans like the time-worn process of pouring sand down a rat-hole? Do the pitifully few graduates represent a true picture of Mexican ability? Do the "drop-outs" mean a failure in our educational, social, and democratic systems, or are they a reflection on the inability of the Mexican to conform, to be assimilated?

The teachers of Mexican children are often told that their efforts in the present cannot be checked or evaluated in the results achieved within the lifetime of the teachers themselves. Most grammar schools are beginning now on the second generation, with the first generation coming out of high school, marrying, and carrying out the tenets they have learned. Will these tenets be the "relatively scientific" ideals of America, or the "superstitious background" of their Indian ancestors?[14] This study proposes to investigate the trend of acculturation as evidenced by the boys and girls included in the unusual group.

---

[14]Bogardus, op. cit., p. 68.

CHAPTER II

CULTURAL BACKGROUNDS

Each individual receives at birth an inheritance of complicated culture patterns, and to this legacy he responds throughout his life. We behave as we do because of the total situation in which we find ourselves.[1] To the patterns in which we are born are added the experiences with which we are surrounded.

In the case of the Mexican in America, the cultural patterns, in simplified form, rise from three main cultural influences: Indian, Spanish, and American. It is the purpose of this chapter to review those patterns which seem pertinent to the study of the unusual Mexican.

Of the Mexican in Mexico, Manuel Gamio says:

> "Generally speaking, to know the conditions under which a people live it is indispensable to know those under which it developed in the past, for to a great extent, the present is to be explained by the past. This is especially true of a people such as the Mexican, formed of an indigenous majority which does not live on a modern plane of civilization, but presents the same or a similar life to that during the colonial period, or even prehistoric times. Though a large part of our natives speak Spanish, their huts or jacales, their domestic utensils such as the metate (corn-grinder), the petate (leaf mat), the huarache (leather sandal), their pagan polytheism, their ideas of witchcraft and magic, etc., are almost identically those of several centuries ago. The archeological-historical evolution of our native population is therefore a necessary postulate to the true comprehension of its living conditions today."[2]

A. Indian Cultural Influences

The cultural influences of the ancient Indian ancestors of the modern Mexican are evident in many forms. Those vestiges that touch the life of the Mexican in America are integral parts of daily living. Perhaps the most persistence evidence is found in the food of the Mexican family, the tortillas, moles, tamales; the use

---

[1]Charles S. Ellwood, "The Cultural or Psychological Theory of Society," Journal of Applied Sociology, Vol. X: p. 12.

[2]Gamio, in Jose Vasconcelos and Manuel Gamio, Aspects of Mexican Civilization (Chicago: University of Chicago Press, 1926), p. 136.

as stapes of beans, maize, chili, squash and tomatoes, and combinations of these. All of these are legacies of centuries of Indian ancestors.[3] The kitchen utensils, ollas, comales, and metates are in use today in even the most "Americanized" home. The use of hard beds without mattresses, or almost no mattress, if one is used, goes back directly to the Indian custom of sleeping on a petate, or rush mat. One informant, when asked about his erect posture, replied, "It is from sleeping on cement floors with very little under me. You Americans sleep too soft; you need comfort, while we need sleep."

The fear of night air has so strong a hold on the mind of the Mexican that only the most "modernized" will open a window for fresh air after sundown.[4] The porters in the hotels in Mexico City will advise against opening windows. The finest rooms have that "closed in" odor so offensive to the fresh air fiend.

The sandals (huaraches) worn by the Mexicans, and recently affected by men and women in the United States, trace directly back to Indian footwear of pre-Columbian days. The poncho worn on cold days by many of our orange pickers was seen throughout ancient Mexico.

These are the outward signs of a culture of long ago. The more subtle evidences of Indian culture are as obvious to the student of the Mexican scene, but far more difficult to trace or to substantiate. Robert N. McLean gives the following list of traits as remainders of Indian culture: The habit of being religious, the mysticism of the Mexican, color and tone sense, innate courtesty, suspicion of motives, inertia, and courage (physical).[5]

E. D. Trowbridge lists the qualities he believes are inherent in the Mexican from his Indian origin, dividing them into faults and abilities. Faults: Does no

---

[3]Robert Redfield, "The Material Culture of Spanish-Indial Mexico," American Anthropologist, N. S., XXI: 616 ff.

[4]Elsie Clews Parsons, Mitla: Town of the Souls (Chicago: University of Chicago Press, 1936), p. 480.

[5]Robert N. McLean, That Mexican! (New York: Fleming H. Revell Co., 1928), pp. 15-29.

thinking for himself, needs restraint, easily led, affectionate and lovable, apt but not quite developed, intellect of a child. Abilities: Initiative, mechanical ability.[6]

Perhaps the best summation of the opinion of Robert Redfield on the question of remaining cultural values is given by Elsie Parsons in her chapter pertaining to Indial culture. She says:

> "Redfield points out that much of the material culture is Indian, i.e., pre-conquest: the house structure, the preparation of food, crops and agricultural methods, weaving and pottery-making, the use of copal gum, the ancient incense, and of several other natural resources, but that in social organization, apart from survival of an ancient subdivision of the town, and in psychological attitudes, the townspeople are Spanish rather than Indian, the psychology and social structure largely European."[7]

Speaking for herself, she continues:

> "Psychological analysis I cannot attempt, as this study is cultural rather than psychological, but on occasion I have referred to psychological attitudes which have appeared to me to partake of Indian rather than European character; the attitude of secretiveness as a protection from ridicule or criticism or interference; the impulse to escape from a situation you do not like rather than to resist it or to reform it; wearing opposition down by repetition or nagging or, as we say, not knowing how to take no for an answer; non-competitiveness and a lack of personal aggressiveness; desire for social peace and unity, and conviction of the need of town solidarity; repugnance to physical contacts; unwillingness to give offense or make an enemy, which includes reticence about other people's affairs, and unwillingness to entertain anger, animosity, or revengefulness, emotions which will make you sick or lead to enmities; fear of making enmities; no manifestation of sexual interest whatsoever, and, finally, taking much more interest in how people behave than in how they feel or think."[8]

In emphasizing the cultural influences of the Indian in Mexico it is well to keep in mind that the Indian of that country has a unique place in the history of pre-Columbian civilization. The history of Mexico is not one of gradual rise of

---

[6]E. D. Trowbridge, Mexico Today and Tomorrow (New York: The MacMillan Co., 1926), p. 17.

[7]Elsie Clew Parsons, op. cit., p. 480.

[8]Parsons, op. cit., p. 480.

cultures and gradual decay. It is rather that of "a process of continuous destruction and substitution of cultures instead of the regular growing and evolving of one period into the other."[9]

As Vasconcelos insists: "Our Indians then are not primitive, as was the Red Indian, but old, century-tried souls who have known victory and defeat, life and death, and all of the moods of history."[10] Thos cultural vestiges that could withstand the battering of repeated assaults must be strong and innate parts of the people who are the inheritors of this legacy.

It is to be seen that there is almost no agreement among the students of the Indian in Mexico as to what constitutes typical Indian characteristics. The results of inquiry are bound to bear the prejudices, beliefs and hopes of the observer. But, unsubstantiated as these suppositions may be, there is a basic truth in them that defies doubt.

Art and music teachers of Mexican children in this country will vouch for the ability of these groups as compared with other racial groups in the American school system. The rise of modern art in Mexico, as evidenced by the schools of Diego Rivera, J. C. Orozco, and R. Montenegro, are tangible proofs of the great heritage of Mexican artists. The color sense, love of warm colors and unusual color combinations are an integral part in the life of the Mexican.

Music and its attendant arts of singing and dancing are the backlog of every Mexican home. There is seldom a Mexican who does not command one of these art forms, and the beauty of the playing and the singing of these self-taught artists springs in part from the influence of Indian ancestors who possessed only the most primitive instruments, but who still created a wealth of folk music.

B. Spanish Cultural Influences

Robert Redfield says, "The Mexican folk are not necessarily Indian. The folk culture is a fusion of Indian and Spanish elements. The acculturation which gave rise to this mixed culture took place three hundred years ago, largely within the

---

[9]Vasconcelos, in Vasconcelos and Gamio, op. cit., p. 4.
[10]Ibid., p. 79.

12

first few generations after the Conquest."[11] With the coming of Cortez and his soldiers of fortune, the centuries of isolation that had engulfed the whole of Mexico came to an end. As Gamio points out, "the immediately succeeding racial contact had no ethical, social, or eugenic tendencies, but was exclusively physical. The white man possessed the native woman wherever and whenever he saw fit. The resultant offspring were the material out of which a new race is being forged."[12]

Vasconcelos asserts that "the mestiso represents an entirely new element in history; for if it is true that in all times the conquered and the conqueror have mixed their bloods, it is also unquestionably true that never before had there come together and combined two races as wide apart as the Indian and the Spanish, and never before had the fusing process of two unrelated breeds intermingling and practically disappearing in order to create a new one."[13]

As with the Indian, the tangible evidences of Spanish culture in the Mexican are to be found in the homely artifacts of daily use. In the clothing worn by the Mexican in America, the reboze or head covering, the straw hat or sombrero, the long full skirt, the use of ear rings in pierced ears, are remnants of Spanish custom. The use of meats in the diet--particularly the use of chicken on festive occasions--the machete or cutting knife, the guitar and cornet are all outward symbols of Spanish influences.

And as with the Indian, the subtle and psychological characteristics stemming from Spanish culture are apparent but equally as difficult to substantiate. The persistence of the indigenous groups in spite of persecution by civil and church law, the continuing resurgence of Indian culture, prolonged and maintained by the Mestizo, all serve to cloud the issue of what is Spanish and what is Indian. When Elsie Clews Parsons was searching for just the right village to study this very problem of the fusion of cultures, she relates that she asked herself:

> "Where could I find helpful comparative clues? Obviously in Latin America, particularly in Mexico, where in tribe upon tribe the process of cultural assimilation has been going on for centuries and in such varying degrees that sometimes the Indian is foremost,

---

[11]Robert Redfield, Tepoztlan, A Mexican Village (Chicago: University of Chicago Press, 1930), p. 13.

[12]Gamio, in Vasconcelos and Gamio, op. cit., p. 40.

[13]Vasconcelos, in Vasconcelos and Gamio, op. cit., p. 83.

sometimes the Spanish. In Mexico surely there would be no lack of touchstones by which to learn what is Spanish, what Indian. But society in Mexico or anywhere else is not a tapestry to pick threads from and expect to find a new design in one's hand; and assimilation is one of the most subtle and elusive of social processes, which does not reveal itself by plucked threads, or by isolated facts."[14]

By a process of elimination it should be simple to prove those things that are derived from Indian culture, and by subtracting them from the Mexican as we see him, to determine that those qualities which remain are of Spanish extraction. The problem is not that simple. The Spanish conquerors, themselves, believed something of the same sort. It is maintained that

"the cultural contact between the Spanish colonist and the native population is of great sociological significance, and deserving of special attention. Immediately upon the conquest of the Indian came his economic ruin; his lands and all valuable possessions passed into the hands of the invader, and he himself became the servant of his conqueror, obliged to work in his mines or estates or pay him tribute. With the Indian effectively subjugated, the Spaniard thought it would be an easy task to blot out the remnant of his autochthonous culture and substitute the civilization imported from Spain. His plan, however, met with utter failure."[15]

It is true that there are cultural evidences of Spanish origin remaining, untouched by fusion with the Indian. The "courting customs" of the Mexican are a direct borrowing from the Spanish. "Hecho el Oso" and "Hecho el Callo" are a part of every romance. That is, courting a girl by standing outside her window and bandying small talk in whispers, or by having friends serenade the senorita with limpid love songs in the early morning while the "would-be Romeo" stands in an entrancing posture of adoration. Many irate Americans can vouch for the persistence of this custom in this country. It has a deeper import than meets the eye. It is the evident sign of the segregation of women.

The place of women in the Spanish scene is one of subservience. There are no famous Mexican women; no infringement on the male prerogative. The custom of segregation has carried over into the school systems in Mexico, and the great majority of young girls and boys never have an opportunity to meet on any common ground. It has been only within the last few years that girls received an

_____

[14]Parsons, op. cit., p. 40.

[15]Vasconcelos and Gamio, op. cit., p. 110.

education of any kind. The church schools gave what religious training was necessary, and little more was required.

The fusion of cultures is most evident in the growth of the "Mexican language," since the Spanish spoken in Mexico is a tongue filled with Indianisms, idions of the indigenous groups, half-changed words and unbelievable pronunciations. The Mexican of today is easily distinguished from Spanish by even the most casual student of the language. Nevertheless, the growth of a common tongue has been an incalculable influence on the fusion of the two cultures.

The common Mexican architectural types, the haciendo, the street-facade, tile roofs, and pleasant patios are of Spanish origin. One of the most significant aspects of Mexican culture is to be found in these. The drab exterior, identical with the next protal, the unpainted gate-way that may repel the uninitiated; but through the doorway a breath of flowers, a murmur of cool water, a small bird pouring out his heart in sunshine, the family gathered about its hearthstone, the patio. The Mexican in America can only express this innate love of a quiet, pleasant place by the "altar-place" in his home and the innumerable pots and jars of flowers ranged from the front porch to the back.

The custom of the siesta was brought from Spain. The "closed-up" look of the Mexican town, large or small, during the afternoon (usually from one until three o'clock) indicates the wide-spread nature of this pleasant custom. The leisurely, heavy noon-day meal is immediately followed by a short nap, or at least a rest, be it in a comfortable bed or rolled in a serape on the ground. The only people on the streets are sure to be doctors answering imperative calls, or American tourists who come to "do" Mexico in fifteen days, side trips included. Travelers in Spain note this same cessation of activity, and perhaps the reason for its continuation in "New Spain" is to be found in the natural propensity of the Indian toward taking life in easy stages and always saving energy for tomorrow.

The influence of the Catholic church, as brought to Mexico by the Jesuit order, played a tremendously important part in the fusion of Indian and Spanish cultures. The Indians were at first considered little better than animals, no rights were accorded them, but with the recognition by the church of their possession of a soul, at the insistence of the then Bishop of the Indes, the unblessed liaisons of the Spanish were frowned upon, and marriage became the rule. The Church demanded the right to protect the resultant children, and in this way a place was made for the Mestizo. In any light, however, the Catholic religion as practiced in Mexico differs as widely from "the pure faith" brought by the "Fathers" as do the native cultures of the two races. The sacred places of the Aztecs are utilized for cathedrals dedicated to a brown-skinned Virgin. So-called miraculous springs are the same under Indian religious custom and that of the Catholic faith of today. The innumerable feast days are a pleasing compromise between Catholic saints' days and the festivals to the sun, rain, and war gods of the Indians.

The custom of a Saint's Day rather than a birthday is again from the Spanish. Boys and girls are usually named for the saint whose day is nearest to that of their birth. It is unusual for a Mexican to celebrate his actual birth date unless the day falls on the date of his name-sake. In the United States very little Mexican children celebrate their Saint's Day, but choose to celebrate their actual birth-day as they become older.

C. American Cultural Influences

The Mexican in America finds life as he has valued it drastically changed. Time for the joy of living is crowded out by the necessity of the pursuit of the dollar. The siesta days are gone, the joyous festivals, the leisurely pace of daily tasks, are bounded by deadliness of "time for work," "time for school," "time for church." The mechanical precision of our life is a never ceasing wonder to the Mexican. Moises Saenz, Minister of Education in Mexico, an educator trained at Columbia and the Sorbonne, says of a trip to the United States:

> "Everywhere I was confronted with the standard, the standard in language, in morals, in food. I traveled in standard trains running on standard time with standard equipment. I was the beneficiary of the standard service of the professional servants. In all the cafeterias of all the towns I visited, I enjoyed food of standard appearance and standard quality. In every city where the train stopped long enough, I bought a paper which always looked the same. There were the same motion picture houses, over-ornate, seventy degrees cool, with their incredibly attired ushers and their syndicated programs. And apparently all the one hundred and twenty million of Americans listen to Amos 'n Andy from six forty to seven p.m."[16]

---

[16]Moises Saenz and Herbert I. Priestley, Some Mexican Problems (Chicago: University of Chicago Press, 1926), p. 40.

16

The strangeness of this new country manifests itself in many ways. The unfamiliar language is the greatest barrier to the Mexican's rapid adaptation. The customs and mores of the Americans are strange to him. The homes and furnishings in many instances are unfamiliar. It is only natural that he feels impelled to move into one of the already established Mexican communities, where ways are more understandable. The Mexican father finds almost his only contact with typical American life in the field of work (he has perhaps an American boss); the mother, in periodic trips to the shops and an occasional visit to the school. Thus the mother and father are able to maintain for themselves the familiar pattern of Mexican ways, but in the second generation the pattern breaks down since the young people go to the American schools and learn to speak, to read and to write the incomprehensible language.

A strange relationship results from the parents' lack of facility with the English language. The parent in Mexico, particularly the father, is the seat of wisdom, the fount of knowledge. In America any one of his brood, with the magical knowledge of English which they possess, can leave him helpless. The positions are reversed and he must learn from his child. This is to him an unnatural situation and the father compensates for his dependence on the child by holding him fast to the "old ways," by demanding more and more obedience in other things. This, in part, accounts for the persistence of the use of Spanish among the second generation Mexicans. However, there are other equally important reasons for not speaking English and not accepting American customs readily. They lie in the feeling of inferiority that is forced on our minority groups, and in the natural resistance to a deprivation of status. When questioned concerning this fact, and reminded of the discourteousness of conversing in an unfamiliar language, the Mexicans reply, "Why should we use English always? To the Americans we are just Mexicans, regardless of how hard we try to be like them. Why should we accept the language and customs of another race when we have our own?"

In contrast with the segregation which obtains in Mexico, the boys and girls sit in the same room, play together on the school ground, join hands in games, and dance together in the school programs. The parents protest and are told that "it is the custom in America; girls and boys should -e together." But the old ones shake their heads and predict dire consequences.

17

The teachers took liberties with the very bodies of their children. They weighed and measured the children. They gave them nasty-tasting medicines from large bottles, and who knew what it would do to them? The school doctor and nurses sent home notices about vaccination. True, the notice was in Spanish; one could at least read it, or find a friend who could, but what of the child who had lost her arm, or died of horrible boils from the poison the doctor put in him? Didn't they know the poison came from horses? Who could make them hurt their children?

There is a club for mothers. The teachers send home notices. It meets in the afternoon. Who is to stay with the babies? Who is to get papa's dinner? What do they do at the club? Sometimes a dentist comes and tells them that for the children's teeth it is good to give each child a quart of milk a day. "Madre de Dios!" Do they not know that milk is precious, that it costs fourteen cents a quart, and that the family has six children, and that papa works for two dollars a day? How can one do what these rich people say? It is easy enough to talk of these things, but who will tell poor people how to make a dollar bill go for shoes and sweaters and food and doctor bills--and then for quarts of milk?

The boys want to go to the picture shows. Every Saturday or Sunday. There they see the bad men that one whispers about in Mexico. Or they see love pictures; kissing and hugging are done right there before them. This is very bad and will make bad girls and boys. American people do not understand how bad this is, for the priest tells them in church that it is bad to see these things, and the American people do not go to church very much.

Sometimes the schools give dances for the young people. The girls are encouraged to go. But at home consternation rules. How are the girls to go? They cannot walk down the streets at night. Papa is tired, but it is out of the question for good girls to go out alone at night; these American do not understand that girls need to be protected. They must stay at home.

The children bring home health charts from school. There are many rules for good health. Good health is a thing close to the heart of every mother. But, "mira!" keep the windows open at night? It is impossible. Do they not know of the diseases that come on the night air? This is not a good rule. Do not drink coffee. What is one to give children that is hot for breakfast? The beans are

18

cold from last night's supper, tortillas are not made for the day. A piece of bread and a cup of hot coffee are filling and warming, and this is more than was ever had in Mexico. What do they want from the "pobres?" Eat leafy vegetables and yellow vegetables. Where is one to find these on the pittance that father earns? What is wrong with beans? What is wrong with corn tortillas? This was the food that all of the ancestors ate. It did not kill them. They are strong. When hard work is to be done the Mexican is called. These rules are good, perhaps, for the rich Americans but for the Mexicans the old way is best.

Then there is the school law that insists that all girls and boys must be in school until they are eighteen. In Mexico the average young couple are well started on their family duties by this time. The boys should be at work long before they are this age; it is not right that they should sit in the school rooms when they are young and strong. Do they want to be professors? It is not good to put too much in the mind. One cannot be happy if one knows too much. As for the girls. These girls will be old maids. No boy wants to marry a girl who knows too much. She will be lazy. All day she will read the paper, even magazines, the house will be dirty, she will have few children, if she does get a husband. There will be few strong backs to make her work light when she is old. These are the old ones. Against this wall of misunderstanding the young Mexican struggles, propelled ever by the school, his American friends, and his observation of American life, interpreted by his understanding of English. The conflict of cultures in the young Mexican is a dual one: first, the conflict of the centuries of racial strain within himself, and the American pattern; and second, the conflict of his understanding of the American pattern, and the firm Mexican mode of life of his parents.

There is a third and even more unsurmountable obstacle. This is the racial prejudice he encounters in America. This is the barrier with which the young Mexican is now brought face to face. It is incomprehensible to him. He struggles to understand, to make himself one with his American classmates, to efface himself, to do his part. He feels as American as John Jones. He likes swing music, Superman, and Bob Hope. He knows the latest words to the latest hit tune, he can rattle off the records of the leading baseball stars, and he gets a lump in his throat when he watches the flag go by in the Armistice Day parade. But, when he goes to get a job, he is told that only "white boys" are being hired.

D. Evidences of Cultural Conflict

It has been said that conflict is determined by attitudes and expressions of attitudes.

> "By conflict is meant a relationship between two groups which involves attitudes of superiority, contempt, prejudice, etc., on the part of the more powerful group toward the weaker group. These attitudes may find open and blatant expression or they may be subtly expressed by a reserve."[17]

Conflict, as experienced by the Mexicans in the Chaffey school district is not of the overt type. Its expression is subtle; almost imperceptible "absent treatment," the lack of expression rather than its active evidence. According to the Mexicans living in the district, they are more nearly free from discrimination here than in any other section of Southern California. Yet in this area admittedly free from bias the Mexican is not wholly admitted into community life; there is a reserve that comes from an attitude of superiority. The public is not impressed by the Mexicans as persons; they lump them all into one group. This group is in most instances stigmatized by the conduct of its most undesirable members. It is common custom to preface a reference to this group by such descriptive adjectives as "dirty, diseased, unresponsive, unintelligent," etc., with no consideration for the individual status of its members.

Little of the prejudice which is expressed against the Mexican is formally organized. The days of the Klu Klux Klan seem to have passed. It is the individual American who fails to understand the individual Mexican. Many times when the unfairness of an attitude is pointed out to him, he immediately expresses regret at his lack of understanding, and explains that it is not malice which prompts him but indifference or lack of information. It is in the unthinking individual that we find the focus of discrimination.

The Chaffey High School and Junior College enjoy a reputation for fair treatment of minority groups. The young people interviewed commented on the splendid treatment accorded them by the teachers and pupils. In only one instance did a

---

[17]Quoted by William Carlson Smith in _Americans in the Making_ (New York: Appleton-Century Co., 1939), p. 234, from L. V. Stonequist, "The Marginal Man: A Study in the Subjective Aspects of Cultural Conflict" (unpublished dissertation, University of Chicago, 1930), p. 307.

boy feel that there might have been prejudice against him on the part of one of the teachers, but he hastened to add that it might have been a clash of personalities rather than racial discrimination. Another boy wrote:

> "I found it a pleasant place and loved it as I should. I had many friends there, and some of my most pleasnat memories come from my years at Chaffey."

Other informants mentioned particular teachers who had had a tremendous influence on their lives, aiding them in crises beyond their duties, and extending their friendship outside of school hours as well as in school. Many of this group mentioned the fact that if it had not been for these gestures of friendship at critical times in their schooldays they undoubtedly would not have been able to continue. Most of the group had been aided through school by funds from the N.Y.A. Its members stated that the authorities went out of their way to make these funds available and to encourage them with this financial assistance. There was no question in the minds of these young people that if "life" were carried on in the same manner as "school," "the world would be a far better place in which to live."

The school, of course, has a responsibility for social adjustment, and makes an effort to secure the acculturation of the Mexican, a responsibility which the business world has not yet generally assumed for its own area of responsibility. It is the occasional flare-up of the open expression of the lack of understanding by the business group which brings the actual treatment of the Mexican in this community before the public eye.

In February 1939, a news story "broke" in the little Spanish newspaper, El Espectador, concerning a Mexican boy of American birth and a companion. The young couple, clean and well-dressed, bought tickets for the picture show in Upland, and walked down the aisle to the center section where they wished to sit. The assistant manager brusquely told them that they would have to sit in one of the seats in the first fifteen rows. The boy protested politely and asked if he had bought the right kind of ticket for the seats in which he wished to sit. The assistant manager replied that it made no difference what kind of tickets he had bought, "all Mexicans had to sit within the first fifteen rows." The young couple left the building and went to Ignacio Lopez, editor of El Espectador, who has made a reputation for himself throughout southern California by his fearless attack on any form of discrimination or prejudice against minority groups. Mr. Lopez wrote stinging accounts in his

21

paper of this open evidence of racial discrimination, and urged that all Mexicans and friends of Mexicans attend a meeting to be held in Upland on the following Sunday.

Hundreds of interested persons went to this meeting and, after being addressed by the Mexican Consul for the San Bernardino district, decided to take action against the theatre in the only peaceable way at their disposal, bringing to the attention of all the business men in the community the amount of Mexican trade they enjoyed, by the use of the boycott. The extent of the support given this effort by fair-minded Americans was gratifying to the Mexicans. An announcement from a theatre manager was soon forthcoming: The policy of the theater would hence-forth be equal treatment for all customers. The incident was closed but the memory survived. For the first time local cases of discrimination had been aired in the public press. The Ontario Daily Report and The Upland News, leading newspapers covering the Chaffey District, carried objective stories of the events, and both papers published editorials on the undemocratic prejudice evidenced by the incident. The Mexican was made to realize that there were Americans who believed in his rights in this country and who stood solidly back of him.[18]

Chaffey Junior College has a swimming pool which is available to the public during the summer months for a small fee. Regulations require each bather to use a shower before entering the plunge, and each must pass before the alert eye of the attendant. One Sunday in the summer of 1939, several Mexican boys (among them three included in this study) went to the pool to enjoy their holiday. When they attempted to buy tickets of admission they were told that Monday was the day re-served for Mexicans. They protested politely, and the attendant admitted that the ruling was not to his liking, but that he was powerless to admit them. The boys, all of whom during school time at Chaffey swam with their classmates, decided to see Ignacio Lopez and determine their rights. Mr. Lopez took the matter up, both in his newspaper and with the school authorities. The incident was brought to a close by the following letter from the Superintendent of the Chaffey Schools, quoted in an article appearing in El Espectador:

---

[18]El Espectador, Ontario, California, February 17, 24, and March 3, 1939.

"My dear Mr. Lopez,

Confirming our conversation of Sunday, I want to state that all American citizens may use the Chaffey plunge on equal terms. Furthermore, all students, whether in day or evening classes, are to receive the same privileges in the enjoyment of the plunge.

"At your request, there will be no special time of the week-- such as Monday morning--when Mexicans are to use the plunge.

"We hope that more and more of our Mexican friends will become citizens of this country, thus making any distinction unnecessary.

"Sincerely,

(Signed) Gardiner W. Spring"[19]

This incident clearly shows that problems of discrimination in the Chaffey community, when pointed out, are rapidly solved in a fair and judicious manner. This cooperation between the Chaffey schools and the Mexican community is an example of the ability of people without bias to settle differences in an amicable way.[20] Mr. Lopez comments on the unusual rapidity and fairness with which the matter was ended:

"Es nuestro regogico el comentar este incidente por el hecho que aqui se ha rendido un gesto de justicia. Es notable que en otras lugares de este Estado se continue abusando de los derechos que asisten a los cuidadanos y de manera sorpendente se segregue y se divida a personas cultas y limpias por ignorancia o prejuicios infundados. Por su acitutud, Chaffey demuestra una vez mas su gran espiritu cooperativo para con nostros."[21]

Further evidence of open expression of the attitude of superiority in this community is found in the experience of another of the boys in this study. He was refused service in a local restaurant and was told to "get out and stay out"; only "white" people were served there. Although this occurrence was not given the publicity that the other cases of discrimination had enjoyed, it has been told about the community, and has caused so much critical feeling against the restaurant owner

---

[19]El Espectador, October 6, 1939.

[20]It might be mentioned that when the Chaffey schools completed the new auditorium the Mexicans of the community planned and carried out an extravagant entertainment, the proceeds from which were donated to a fund for Mexican costumes for the ushers. It was a gesture heartily appreciated by the whole community.

[21]El Espectador, October 6, 1939.

that the place is jokingly called the "out of state" restaurant since it has so little local trade. This is the only case of refusal of service to occur in this community, but the informants related many similar instances, all of which had occurred in other localities.

Without doubt the greatest discrimination against the Mexican comes in his effort to find a job. At the present time, when the war is our greatest consideration, when newspapers and radios carry urgent appeals for skilled and unskilled workers to prepare themselves to take their places in industry, the whole group of Mexican mechanics finds it almost impossible to get into the war industries. Only in San Diego is there any opportunity to work in the aircraft plants. The Consolidated Company has opened its doors to all American citizens, regardless of racial background, and is accepting high school graduates with from five to ten weeks of retraining.

The other plants, when asked by the retraining department of the Chaffey "Peoples College" why they persistently refuse to take highly skilled and well recommended Mexican workers, while accepting not as well qualified "American" workers, replied that it is not the policy of the company, but the inability of the workmen already in their employ to get along with Mexican laborers, that dictates refusal to employ them. After receiving assurance that Mexicans would not be hired in the defense industries it was thought advisable not to retrain more of the Mexican boys and girls. However, since the Consolidated Aircraft Company of San Diego has made the first openings for Mexican employment, the Chaffey evening classes have begun to admit Mexicans again, with the hope of placing them in active war work.

CHAPTER III

FACTORS IN THE PROCESS OF ACCULTURATION

A. Family Backgrounds

Migration

The sources of Mexican immigration as tabulated by Manuel Gamio are predominantly the "mesa central," or central plateau, and in lesser proportion the "mesa del norte," or northern plateau. He says: "Guanajuato, Jalisco, and Michoacan, places of mild climate, are the principal contributors, though it would seem that the states of Sonora, Chihuahua, and Nuevo Leon, which, because they are near the border, are advantageously situated for emigration to the United States, and where the climate conditions are more nearly like those in the United States, are also principal contributors."[1]

In the material gathered for this thesis the immigration tends to parallel Gamio's findings.

State	Number	Percent
Total	74	100
Jalisco	26	36
Zacatecas	15	20
Guanajuato	9	12
Michoacan	8	11
Chihuahua	6	8.5
Mexico D.F.	2	1.5
Sinaloa	1	1
United States (one parent born here)		
Texas	1	
California	1	

In like manner the years of entry into the United States seem to parallel general Mexican immigration since 1900.

---

[1]Manuel Gamio, Mexican Immigration to the United States (Chicago: University of Chicago Press, 1930), p. 17.

Year of Entry	Number	Percent
Total	37	100
1900	2	5.5
1901		
1902		
1903		
1904		
1905	1	2.5
1906		
1907		
1908	2	5.5
1909	1	2.5
1910	3	8.5
1911		
1912	3	8.5
1913	1	2.5
1914	1	2.5
1915	1	2.5
1916	10	27.5
1917	1	2.5
1918	3	8.5
1919	4	11
1920	1	2.5
1921		
1922	1	2.5
1923	1	2.5
1924		
1925		
1926	1	2.5

As can be seen from the above table, immigration for this group reached its peak from 1916 to 1919. From the girls and boys interviewed it has been ascertained that the parents were motivated by the desire to escape from the revolution raging in Mexico in those years,[2] and at the same time by the siren song of the American

---

[2]One informant relates his experience at this time (1916) with the formidable Pancho Villa. The informant was a blacksmith in a small village in the state of Jalisco, and, plying his noisy trade, had failed to hear the signal every village used to warn its men to hide so that they would not be forced into one or the other of the fighting groups. He realized his error only when he found himself face to face with the bewhiskered "Panchito." Villa asked him if he knew how to repair harness, and the very frightened blacksmith assured him that there was no better repair man in all Mexico, but that he was a slow and careful worker who would nee much time. This did not seem to displease Villa, who arranged to return for his gear the following morning. In the meantime the blacksmith, who knew no more about harness work than his youngest child, gathered his family together, and in the dark of night set out on the long journey through the lines of both Villa and Carranza. He relates that the greatest risk lay in the constant necessity to guess which

capitalists who were providing, in some instances, free transportation, free living quarters, or using other inducements to urge cheap labor to flow into the United States.[3] It is to be remembered that the world situation then in some ways resembled that of the present time. Unskilled laborers in the United States were being retrained to become semiskilled laborers, consequently there was a shortage of the "hewers of wood and the drawers of water." This need was filled by importation of the strong workers from Mexico.

El Paso was the most usual port of entry into the United States. It is the natural outlet for the great plateau sections of Mexico. The one family entering

Total in Study	37
El Paso, Texas	27
Nogales, Arizona	7
San Ysidro, California	1
Eagle Pass, Texas	2

at San Ysidro, sailed from the port of Acapulco in 1908, and landed at Ensenada, finishing the trip to the border by horse-drawn stage. Without exception the other families came by train.

Of the boys and girls tabulated, only eight made the trip with their parents. All the others have been born in this country since the families arrived. As birth in this country entitles the child to citizenship, it is to be seen that the large majority of the group under discussion are American citizens, a fact to be kept in mind throughout this study.

Total in Study	37
Born in United States	29
Born in Mexico	8

---

arm band was appropriate when meeting bands of roving soldiers. But that he guessed right is attested by the fact that two of his boys are included in this study of unusual Mexicans.

[3]Refer to Immigration figures, Chapter I, p. 5.

Employment Movements

The employment history of many of the immigrant fathers follows a typical pattern. While some of them were small merchants, owning small stores or trading businesses, shoemakers, blacksmiths, and carpenters, the majority of them had been born and raised on the large haciendas, and had spent their youth in agricultural pursuits. (For this latter group the transition to fruit picking, pruning, and orchard care in this country was not such a difficult one.) The pattern of migration differs only as to time, but in the jobs found in the United States the similarity persists. These were either on the railroads or in the mines in Arizona or Texas, and when employment failed in those states, migration was continued on to California for work in the fruit or related industries.

Only one man had during his lifetime a position of importance in industry. He was a paymaster for the large sugar beet factory at one time located in Chino, California. One other father was able to follow his livelihood in this country after migrating. He was a Baptist minister and came to this country expressly to work among the Mexican immigrants who, as he said, "had shown the adventurous spirit necessary to the breaking down of a custom as long fixed as Catholicism." One father was able to learn cement construction work soon after his arrival, and as his sons finished school and joined him, he built up a cement business of his own which is still quite successful. One father, in desperation, went as far as his money would permit, which happened to be San Bernardino, and the first Mexican he encountered told him of the possibility of a job in a new little town at that time just starting, Fontana. He asked for a job the next day and was given one with a construction gang in water pipes for the Union Water Company of the Fontana Farms. That was twenty-six years ago, and when Fontana recently celebrated its Twenty-Fifth Anniversary Jubilee, this man was one of the honored guests, since he had continued in different capacities with the same company for all of that time. Another father began work as a track worker with the Santa Fe in 1912, and has remained with the company, having advanced to the position of a mechanic. Still another was able, with the help of his older sons, to buy three trucks and engage in his own trucking and hauling business. These cases, however, are unusual. The average father has been, or still is, a laborer in the fruit crops in the vicinity of his home, and has been able to do all that has been necessary for his family on what he has earned in this way.

There has been singularly little moving about. The move from Arizona or Texas to California has been in most families the only move. The great majority of them still live in the same community to which they came at that time. In answer to the question, "Why did the family move," the reply was, without exception, "To get a better job." There can be no other consideration when children must be fed and clothed, and a roof provided for the family.

Size and Structure of the Family

The typical family among these unusual Mexicans consists of a father, mother, and 6.05 children.

		Number of Children										
	Total	1	2	3	4	5	6	7	8	9	10	13
Normal home	21		5	1	2	1	2	1	4	1	2	2
Fatherless	9			1	1	2	1	2	2			
Motherless	5						2	3				
Headed by grandmother	2	1			1							
6.05 children per family	37	1	5	2	4	3	5	6	6	1	2	2

In the one family in which there is an only child the informant states that the mother died soon after his birth. He was then raised by his grandmother and had little contact with his father. One other boy was left an orphan in his teens and had been raised by his grandmother with the financial assistance of an older brother. Another boy relates that after the death of his mother and the subsequent remarriage of his father, he was able to establish a home of his own by obtaining work after school and on Saturdays and Sundays. He says that it is not the best system in the world but that it has made him more determined than ever to become a teacher so that he can have "the home of his dreams" some day. In several instances the older brothers and sisters are the support of the family, in some cases helping out financially even after they are married and supporting their own families. One boy stated that the necessity of supporting the family after the death of his father was responsible for the inability of his older brother to continue his education. He said, "He was much smarter than I am; he would have been a credit to the Mexican race, but he was older than me (sic) so he had to give up his school and

29

get a job." Many times this feeling of the sacrifice of the older brothers and sisters was mentioned.

Of the group, four are the sole support of their families, usually in fatherless homes, while five partially support their families, with the help of older brothers and sisters. Eight of the group are married and maintain their own homes, three of the boys assisting at the same time to maintain the family home. The double burden of two homes has in two instances accounted for the inability of the young people to progress beyond high school, in spite of their desire to do so.

Of the eight young people in the study who are married only four have children.

	Total	Size of Family			
Couples	8	4	2	1	1
Children	7	0	1	2	3

The young man who has three children, married soon after his graduation from high school in 1932. The boy with two children was married in 1934. This record as compared with the record of the parents gives an average per family of 1.6 children as against 6.05 children per first generation family. Compared with the average family of the United States, shown by the figures of the 1940 census to have 3.8 members, the second generation Mexicans with families included in this study average 3.6, or 0.2 less than the national average.

While the length of the second generation marriages is not yet long enough to be compared with the marriages of the first generation group, and while the number of second generation marriages is not yet large enough to permit a generalization, it seems that the limitation of families is among the mores which have been adopted.

Nature of the Home

To judge the Mexican home by the exterior is a common error among Americans. To label a district as "Mexican town" is an accepted practice, and differences in the social services, police methods, and the other aspects of public administration are made accordingly. There the tag-ends of homes are left to fade still farther into oblivion, the cheap shacks stuck together in the days when the Mexican was being urged to enter our country, the homes that have seen better days and are patched to serve as a roof and "bed-place"; the made-over stores, added on, reshaped; the houses that began as one-room shelters, and that now twist and turn amazingly with the sides and rooms built on from time to time. These are the exteriors of the homes of our unusual Mexicans. There are no startling differences in the homes among these few. The home of any one of them is next door to all the other houses in the community. With only two exceptions, all of those in the study are located in the "Mexican towns" of the respective communities.

To establish a standard for determining the type of home from which the people under discussion come, it is necessary to base any description on a Mexican standard, rather than on the accepted standard of American homes. The classes are rated as excellent, good, fair, and poor, and all of the homes visited were placed in one or another of these categories. This arbitrary division, however, has taken into consideration not only the exterior, but has included the interior furnishings, accommodations, and possession of the so-called luxuries.

Under accommodations, the principal consideration has been the indoor toilet and bathing facilities. The luxuries have included the possession of a car, a radio, an electric or gas refrigerator, a piano, and subscription to English or Spanish newspapers or magazines. These are of course only outward signs of a standard, but are almost the only means of determining its level.

The homes observed were well furnished, simply and in good taste. There were none of the usual gaudy calendars. In two of the homes there were small spinet-type pianos, and almost all of the homes had a radio, ranging from the most modern short-wave sets to the "midget" type. The floor coverings ranged from scrubbed boards, through linoleum rugs, to broadloom carpet; furniture from modern over-stuffed to simple board chairs and "day-beds." The atmosphere was definitely American rather than Mexican, and the homes were clean and neat, although the families were not expecting to be observed at the time.

Total in Study   37

Toilet		Bath	
In	Out	In	Out
29	8	33	4

31

Luxuries

Total in Study	37
Spanish newspaper	32
Radio	30
English newspaper	20
Refrigerator (gas or electric)	15
Magazines	13
Piano	12

On the basis of this standard the homes fall into the following classifications:

Total Homes	37
Excellent	8
Good	9
Fair	10
Poor	10

Home Ownership

The typical Mexican is buying his own home. It seems to be an established habit to buy a home as soon as possible, all of the members of the family contributing, and then in turn buying homes for themselves as soon as possible. There is a note of pride in the voice when they answer the question about home ownership. Many of them use the old phrase: "A poor thing but mine own." This fact explains, in part, the custom of families doubling up, or the young couple living in the husband's family home until such time as they may be able to purchase a home of their own.

Total Homes	37
Own own home	33
Renting	3
Living in Company house	1

B. Color

It was hoped that a study of the ethnic background of the unusual Mexican could be included in this thesis, but the lack of knowledge on the part of the family as to its antecedents was soon evident. Many informants had heard that they had a Spanish grandfather, or an Irish grandmother, and supposed there must be "some other kind of blood in their family because they were so light." As for family trees, however, none were to be found. Each of the persons interviewed was well aware of the Indian blood in his veins, some boasting that "there was not a drop of any other kind." And each was only too well aware of the color line that has been drawn in the United States.

For the purpose of classification, three color groups have been distinguished: Light, medium, and dark. These are not easy to describe but, in further clarification, a light Mexican can be considered to have the approximate coloring of the accepted "Latin type," the medium Mexican the warm shade of deep olive, and the dark Mexican quite brown, with the bronze tint of the American Indian. According to this classification, the unusual Mexicans were grouped in the following way:

Total in Study	37
Light	8
Medium	19
Dark	10

As a background the coloring is far more important than any consideration of "blood heritage" among other groups. Without doubt, if the Mexican could have his dearest wish it would be to be white. The white man in his country and in America has made the Mexican superconscious of his color. To succeed in America with the handicap of color is to surpass the "Horatio Alger" stories of our parents. Without exception, the Mexican who was medium or dark had many stories to relate of racial discrimination. They are banned from public swimming pools, refused service in many restaurants, forced to sit in separate sections in picture shows and at concerts, and in many instances not permitted even to apply for jobs. The equality they have been accorded on drivers' licenses, draft registration cards, and in the census, in the space marked "race," has had a splendid effect on their morale. They are classed as White.

The unthinking public, which flaunts that precious word, must not have heard of the fifteen hundred shades of white discernable to the naked eye. To be told that there is no employment should be sufficient, but to have it specified that only "white" boys or girls need apply is to receive the ultimate insult. The constitution of the United States guarantees the right of franchise, regardless of "race, color, or previous condition of servitude." The Social Security laws and the policies of the Labor Relations Board are based on the assumption that all men

33

are indeed "created equal." In actual practice the truth tends in a far different direction. But these young people are not cynics; they are realists. The boys who look ahead to joining some branch of military service hope that in the willingness they show to give their lives for a country which has not always practiced what she preached, they may be assuring for the Mexicans who come after them a better and fairer opportunity.

One informant, now with the army, wrote in reply to enquiries about the problem of the Mexican:

> "Sometime in the future, when and if this war is over, I am going to delve into this problem, heart and soul. This problem is to me now secondary. It wasn't before Pearl Harbor, but now it is. With the world plunged into a titanic struggle and the pent-up hatred of years unleashed, providence only knows what the final outcome will be; but regardless of the outcome of this war, you may rest assured that all of the boys of Mexican origin now serving, and all of the men in the armed forces, will never live to see the time when surrender is the order of the day."

The desire to succeed, among this unusual group, stems in some degree from the knowledge of the part they inadvertently play as representatives of the Mexican people. They often mentioned that they were the only Mexican members of clubs in high school, and that they felt that their American associates had "changed their minds" about the Mexicans when they discovered that they were acceptable members of the club. It is to be hoped that these young leaders may have influenced many of the American group so that the role of the Mexican may become one of equal standing in later generations. In no case did one of the Mexicans harbor resentment against his former classmates.

C. Economic Backgrounds

Actual figures covering family income for this group it was impossible to obtain. Had the study been in progress over a length of time, several of the families could have been persuaded to have kept budgets. Without this aid, figures on budgets would be little better than guess work. No definite figures were asked or given, but evidence of the presence or absence of income was apparent. The evidence of a higher material standard was plainly seen in some homes, which evidently benefited from many contributors, while in others the lack of income was shown by the limitation of furnishings and luxuries.

Of the studies made of the income of Mexican workers in California, and more especially in southern California, one preceded the depression and the other coincided with the onset of the depression. These are cited because it may be assumed that they are applicable to the Chaffey Mexican community, a group of permanently settled Mexicans, whose incomes are more stable than those of other Mexican families.

The first study was made for Governor C. C. Young by his Mexican Fact-Finding Committee.[4] It reports that at the time the study was made, in the years 1928 and 1929, and covering 435 families in southern California, forty-seven percent of them had incomes of $1,000 or less, fifty-three percent had incomes of $1,000 or more during the consecutive months for which their incomes were reported.

Table II

Total Twelve Months Income	Number	Percent	Cumulative Percent
Total	435	100	
Less than $300	11	2.5	2.5
$300 to $400	8	1.8	4.3
$400 to $500	22	5.8	9.4
$500 to $600	27	6.2	15.6
$600 to $700	26	6.0	21.6
$700 to $800	34	7.8	29.4
$800 to $900	38	8.7	38.1
$900 to $1,000	39	9.0	47.1
$1,000 to $1,100	36	8.3	55.4
$1,100 to $1,200	36	8.3	63.7
$1,200 to $1,300	36	8.3	72.0
$1,300 to $1,400	15	3.4	75.4
$1,400 to $1,500	14	3.2	78.6
$1,500 and over	93	21.4	100

The second study is contained in the report of the Heller Committee for Research in Social Economics, University of California, How Mexicans Earn and Live.[5] The committee states: "To say that they (the Mexican group) are a typical and

---

[4]Mexicans in California, Report of Governor C. C. Young's Mexican Fact-Finding Committee (State Building, San Francisco, California, October 1930).

[5]Cost of Living Studies V: How Mexicans Earn and Live, University of California, Heller Committee for Research in Social Economics (Berkeley: University of California Publications in Economics, XIII: No. 1, 1933).

representative sample of the wage-earning group in the United States, or in the state, would be to add a guess to certainties." But, as has been pointed out, since many of the same conditions exist in the San Diego district and in the Chaffey district (certain of the qualifications for the one hundred families placing them in like circumstances),[6] the study may be considered as at least pointing out possible spread of income for the group under discussion. The survey was conducted in the San Diego district and included one hundred families. The material was gathered between the years 1929 and 1930. The average family income is placed at $1,085.41 to $2,800. These figures do not include the income contributed by the children.

It can be seen that the spread of income varies by family, and that each family has to adjust itself to its own rate of income. It is much the same for the families in this study. Some of the boys and girls said that they were given all the money they needed to complete school, while others said that they had to quit school for a semester now and then in order to be able to continue on what they could save while working. Since the advent of the National Youth Administration, the young people have been able to work and attend school at the same time. Many of the students involved in this study had to help their families during the summer months by working in the fields or packing plants. Almost all of them mentioned experience in some of these activities. In all of the families money was respected, but in some families the lack of money was more acute than in others.

D. Social Patterns

The typical Mexican family is a very closely knit unit. The blood ties, the pride of race, the economic cooperation, serve to bind the family together. The members are not merely unattached individuals; they have their place in the "family solidarity."[7] This solidarity consists of acceptance of financial obligations toward the family, as well as obedience to the head of the family. The father controls the family, makes its decisions, manages the money contributed by the members, and assumes the role of patriarch. The mother is the household manager, rearing the

---

[6]Ibid., pp. 2-6.

[7]William I. Thomas and Florian Znaniecki, The Polish Peasant in Europe and America (Chicago: University of Chicago Press, 1918), p. 89.

children and maintaining the home, a task made more difficult by the numbers of children and the lack of sufficient income. The children must share the arduous tasks of the mother. They are taught to assist in the care of younger children, and to aid by assuming responsibility at an earlier age than is usual among other groups. The Mexican family seldom gathers together around the table for meals, the size of the family making it in most cases impossible. The father and older boys are served first, then the younger children are fed and, after everyone else has eaten, the mother and older girls find time for their meal. This arrangement is not conducive to conversation and the exchange of ideas. The family meets as a group only in the evenings before the children go to bed. The young people in school often mention the lack of privacy for study, as well as the scarcity of study materials in the home.

The sleeping facilities are, in most homes, meager. The children sleep together in one room, often three in a bed, sometimes on pallets on the floor. The young people in this study, however, said that they had better sleeping arrangements in their homes, and that, as the family acquired more income, rooms were added or larger homes were acquired, permitting more privacy.

Wash day in the Mexican home is a day of drudgery. For most families it means the lighting of a fire in the yard, the heating of water in the old-fashioned galvanized tub, the use of a rubbing board, and clouds of steam followed by backaches from the labor expended on dirty overalls and the play clothes of the children. It is small wonder that the very first money that can be spared goes to buy an electric washing machine. Several families will often combine to buy a washing machine and take turns on the monthly payments. Cars are many times purchased in the same manner, all of the members of the family who are able saving to meet the set payments in turn. There is no feeling of "that is mine because I made the most payments on it." The policy is to "share and share alike."

It is the custom of the family to stay at home. An occasional "show," or a shopping trip, with weddings and christening festivals as rare treats, is the usual pattern. When the young people begin to join clubs in high school the parents often feel that they are breaking away from the family. It is most unusual for girls to be permitted to attend evening affairs. The parents resent teachers who attempt to point out the innocence of school gatherings, and only occasionally are parents able to break away from the typical attitude of their neighbors, and permit their daughters to attend school functions. In some cases the parents are looked upon by members of the community as lax in their duties to their children for this broad-mindedness.

The family home is the center of activity. Most of the young people have specified tasks to do when they come from school; after these are accomplished, the home settles down for the night. Early retiring and early rising is the order. The next day goes as the day before, with Saturday night the one night when the family attends some diversion, and Sunday usually set aside for church going and visiting. This simple pattern is irksome to the young people attending our secondary schools and makes them all the more conscious of the difference between their homes and those of their American schoolmates. So strong is the habit of obedience to the father, however, that open rebellion is infrequent. The young people say that it is easier and happier to try to show their parents that the American ways are not bad, only misunderstood.

The common conception of American ways is graphically illustrated by one Mexican father who says: "I am told that becoming an American means being progressive, but if it means that my daughter will bob her hair, disobey her parents, smoke, drink, and be cut until all hours of the night, elope, and finally get divorced, I do not want progress. Our customs may be of the old world, but they suited our parents and they suit us."[8]

It is not this type of parent who has permitted his daughter to attend the secondary schools, although the most lenient Mexican father is most careful of his daughter's reputation, since her happiness depends on her standing in the community. But the old ways are cracking, and each generation is permitted more liberties than the last. As one girl said, "I wish I were my own daughter. Wouldn't I go places and do things like my American friends do!"

The religious pattern in the group was surprising in respect to the number of Protestants. Mexico is supposed to be Catholic, yet more than one fourth of this group was found to be Protestant.

---

[8]Quoted from Jovita Gonzalez de Mireles, "Latin Americans," from Our Racial and National Minorities, edited by Francis Brown and Joseph Roucek (New York: Prentice-Hall, 1939), p. 504.

```
Total in Study      37
Catholic            27      72.9%
Protestant          10      27.1%
```

One young man is working on a ranch and at the same time studying to become a Protestant missionary to Mexico. It is his belief that to go back to Mexico and convert the back-country people to Protestantism is his "call" in life. The father of one girl was a Congregational minister, while the brother of another girl is pastor of a Baptist church. The Catholic members grade themselves as good, fair, and poor Catholics. Those who classify themselves as good Catholics say that they attend all religious ceremonies, and belong to the C.Y.O., the Catholic Youth Organization. The ones who classify themselves as fair Catholics attend mass only occasionally and confession infrequently, while those who consider themselves poor Catholics say that they were baptized Catholic so "they guess they are." When questioned as to whether they would be married in the Catholic church, most of this latter group said it depended upon whom they married. One boy frankly said, "No." It wouldn't make him any more married than to be married by a judge.

Even in those families in which religion played a larger part, the usual house altar was not in evidence. In only one home was even a small shrine to be seen, but in many of the homes there were religious pictures on the walls of the front room. It is to be surmised, from this evidence, that the old ways are changing and that the young people are adopting a less obvious expression of religious feeling. At least, outward symbols are not apparent.

E.   Comparison of Job Placement

The unusual Mexican is proving himself more than normally different from his countrymen in the kinds of employment he is finding.[9] Only a few of the group concerned have the type of job commonly regarded as work for Mexicans; that is, unskilled labor such as fruit picking, pruning, and day labor, the work in which their fathers have engaged. Two boys who have recently graduated from Chaffey explained that they knew they would have to begin their army service soon, and for

---

[9]A table of the occupations of each member of the study group appears at the end of this chapter.

that reason had taken jobs picking lemons as a means to a good daily wage. They
intend to save all the money they can, so that they may be able to supplement their
small army pay, as they can expect no help from home once they are in the service.
Both had promising records at Chaffey, and intend to make use of their education
in doing other work when the war ends.

Each girl and boy in the study qualified the answer to the question relating to
present position by some pertinent revelation as to the road that led him to the
type of job in which he was engaged. The two young men who are in ranch work stated
that their interest in ranching began in Chaffey when they became members of the
"Future Farmers" club. They were particularly impressed with the farm machinery
available for their use, and stated that it was their greatest delight to enter the
tractor-driving contests conducted at the time of the "Chaffey Fair" in the spring
of each year. Both boys specialized in agriculture, as they were certain that they
wanted to enter ranch work. However, they were determined that they would not be
satisfied with day labor, and they worked toward grades that would help them in
obtaining positions of some importance. One of these boys is in charge of all of
the tractor workers on a large ranch near Fresno, while the other is in charge of
a ranch near Etiwanda, California, managing it for an absentee landlord.

One boy, by dogged persistence, was able to obtain a position with the Consolidated Aircraft Company in San Diego. This feat antedates the company's present
policy toward Mexicans by some months. He states that when he had completed his
retraining course in welding and machineshop in the National Youth Administration
training school in San Bernardino, he was a member of a group that was interviewed
by a representative of the Consolidated Aircraft Company. He says that he alone,
out of the group, was not encouraged to apply for work, although he was certain
that his work in the school had been satisfactory, and adds that he was the only
Mexican in the group. When he questioned the retraining teacher as to the possibility of this being discrimination, the teacher urged him to make an attempt to
get a job, regardless of the attitude of the company's representative. This he did.
He took what money the family could spare and made arrangements to stay in San
Diego for two weeks. Each morning he stood in the line waiting before the employment window. When he arrived at the window the agent would say, "There is no work
for you today." Then the youth would step out of line and watch the other men
going in through the gate--American men who had stood in line behind him. After he

40

was certain that men were being hired, and that his color was the barrier, he went back to the end of the line and repeated his request for work, receiving the same reply each time he appeared at the window. It was on the ninth day of the repetition of this proceeding that the employment agent commented on his "staying power," remarking that "anybody who wants a job as bad as you do should get one." He sent the boy inside to see one of the personnel directors, with a memorandum which the boy supposes was the story of his persistence, and after reading the note, questioning the boy on his background, and inspecting his birth certificate, the director hired him. The informant says that there were a few other Mexican employees at that time but that they did not work together, and that the team spirit that is built up in the various branches of the company is not split on racial lines. He feels that it is the opportunity of his life to break down prejudice against the Mexicans "by always doing his part and then a little bit more."

One young Mexican is in his first year at the University of California, studying to become a chemical engineer. According to his statement, his interest in chemistry began in the physics class in Chaffey High School. He was overcome with a desire to do something in the field of research, and says that he became the "terror of the laboratory classes," keeping his teachers and classmates in a state of perpetual fear at the "messes" he continuously concocted. His classmates, on the other hand, relate that more often than not he was to be found at all hours in the Chem. Lab., having forgotten to go to other classes, to eat, or to return home, until the janitor reminded him that it was time to lock up the room. They say that he is a genius, and that some day not only the Mexicans will be proud of him but that all of our country will know of his work. His teachers agree that he is unusually apt in chemistry.

Another group of these boys is attending Chaffey Junior College at the present time. Two of them are enrolled in the civil pilot training corps, which is a new departure in training at Chaffey. This is a separate school conducted at Silver Lake, California, where flying conditions are at their best. It is under the sponsorship of Chaffey system, and regular Junior College classes are carried on in conjunction with ground school and basic training in aeronautics. These boys will be eligible for induction into the Army Air Force upon attaining the required age and the completion of their courses.

Another member of this group is specializing in merchandizing, with the hope of doing business with the Latin-American countries. He is also majoring in Spanish, learning the business and "polite" forms that will be useful to him. He has in the past year constructed a small store in his little community, stocked it, and with the assistance of his sister run it at a small profit. He explains that it is an "experiment in experience." His father was able to advance him the necessary financial assistance, and he has made regular payments on this obligation while keeping current bills paid promptly. His plans for the immediate future call for a small "Malt Shop" to be added to his present store building, an experiment in the "Americanization" of his community. He is also a member of the Claremont Coordinating Council and an active member of the Mexican Y.M.C.A. He belongs to a group which sponsors dances, plays, and sports activities in his Mexican community, and he says that the young people are beginning to enter into constructive leisure time activities.

Still another of the boys attending Chaffey Junior College is an outstanding art student. He has a weekly black and white picture in the school paper, on some topic of current importance. His family was under the impression that he was being given a scholarship in the Chouinard Art School in Los Angeles, in recognition of his exceptional talent. Some of his drawings displayed in the home are of unusual clarity, of decided artistry, and show a well developed artistic personality. He has been encouraged in his special interest since the grammar grades, and he says that his teachers deserve the credit, if there is any, for his success.

The one Mexican girl now attending Junior College is taking the secretarial course, while earning most of her money for clothes, books, and incidentals through the National Youth Administration. She hopes to be able to take a civil service examination when she finishes in June, and to get a position with the government in one of the defense departments.

The last of the Junion College students is planning to become a teacher. He aspires to teaching in the Junior High School grades, as he feels that he would be of the greatest benefit to young Mexican boys and girls of that crucial age group. He has arranged with the young Mexican boy now in the University of California to take over his part-time jobs as soon as he leaves Berkeley, as the departure of the latter will coincide with the other's arrival there. The jobs consist of work that will guarantee his room and board.

42

Of the young men in the armed forces, two have become noncommissioned officers. One is a Staff Sergeant in the Signal Corps at March Field, and is able to
use his commercial training in his capacity as secretary to the Commanding General.
The other is in the clerical department of the Air Corps, Third Air Base, in
Albuquerque, New Mexico. This young man has recently been promoted to the rank of
Corporal, and is in charge of the "paper" work in the maintenance of a large fleet
of trucks. The other boys say that they are "just privates," but that they have
hopes of becoming officers before they are discharged. One of these boys is serving
in Australia, and two others are still in training. The group is soon to be joined
by another member who plans to enlist in the Marines before the end of the summer.
He expects the Marines to be job enough for the time but hopes to gain colorful
experiences so that when he has opportunity he may write stories, which he can sell.
He states that while in Chaffey he had a column called "Strokes and Strides" in the
high school publication, and that he enjoyed something of a reputation with the
student body for this ability. His teachers have encouraged him to go on with his
education, but since his induction into the army is so imminent, he feels that to
get as much experience as possible will stand him in good stead until such time as
he may be able to continue, in some way, his desire to write.

One of the young men who graduated in 1932, found himself facing a world at
the bottom of the depression. He states that he had hoped to continue through
Junior College, but that his family desperately needed all the financial aid available, and that, as they had made repeated sacrifices to enable him to complete
high school, he did not have the heart to refuse them at a time of need. He found
work with a neighbor who built small houses on contract, and in a few months, by
combining the training he had received in the woodshop at Chaffey with the more
practical experience of the new job, plus a great deal of native ability, he became
a finish carpenter. He says that at all times he was able to find work at his
craft, and that for three years he was successful in contracting himself to build
houses, hiring all the additional help that he needed. He has recently removed to
Upland, and hopes to enter a retraining class so that he may qualify for defense
work, and in this way find a useful place in the country's war effort.

A young man who manages a store in the Ontario Mexican community finds that
his ability to use both Spanish and English has been of great benefit to him. The

43

proprietor of the store is Spanish and, since he does not speak English, he permits the young man to conduct all of the buying from the English-speaking salesmen, whereby he learns the essentials of the business. The proprietor depends on the young man and has requested that he be put down as manager, since he, in fact, runs the enterprise.

One boy left his community to obtain better work, and was able through the intercession of a friend to find a position with the May Company in Los Angeles. Beginning as a sock-room clerk, he soon rose to be head clerk in that department, as all of the other employees were called in the draft or had enlisted in the army. Later he was made a salesman in the drapery department, again as a result of the shortage of trained men, and finds that he enjoys his position. He feels, however, that he is shirking his patriotic duty, but as he is the main support of his family, his father being in poor health, he probably will not be called for active duty with the army. Since he had outstanding grades in machine shop, and a great deal of skill in that field, he believes that he should be making use of this ability for the welfare of his country. He attempted to get a job with each of the aircraft companies in the Los Angeles district, but was turned away from every plant without even the satisfaction of being told why he was not employed. He has just learned of the action of the Consolidated Aircraft Company, and hopes to be able to apply there for war work. He would, of course, like the May Company to extend some assurance of the opportunity to resume his position with them, once this emergency has passed, since he realizes that he is learning a great deal, in his capacity as salesman, about the "nicer" things in life.

The boy who is employed as a washer in a laundry regards the job as temporary, until he can complete a retraining course. He has been handicapped by the lack of a birth certificate. Although a native born American, like so many other Americans, he has no legal evidence of that fact. The United States government has recently decided that affidavits of birth, when properly notarized and filed, shall be considered legal evidence of birth. The boy has this affidavit and feels encouraged by the prospect of obtaining a position in defense work. Transportation has always been his great problem. The family does not have a car, and lives far off the main highway that leads to the Chaffey community. He has had to depend on chance rides and, on some occasions, to walk the six miles to and from Chaffey to attend the night classes after a day spent in the water and steam of the laundry. He says that if he can do his bit in this way it has not been too hard a task.

Another of the young men attended a barber college after his graduation from Chaffey, and has had a shop of his own for some time. He is at present retraining for defense work, and he expects to be employed soon in a small plant near his home in Azusa.

The young women are divided, as is almost any group of women of their age, into those who work and those who are housewives. The housewives felt that their days of "leisure" were soon to come to an end. One of the girls who graduated last June, married just after commencement and established a home with her new husband only to have it disrupted by his induction into the army in October. She has not seen him since, and when their baby arrived last month she says that she "just sent him an announcement like everybody else, because he has been gone so long it would be news to him anyhow." She plans to find work when she is able, making use of the secretarial training obtained in high school, as she does not want to be a burden on her parents, with whom she has been living since her husband was called. She remarked, "I can't very well manage on twenty-one dollars a month; besides, with codliver oil, Pablum, and special baby soap, my husband will just about be able to support the baby and not me."

One of the other girls resigned in February from the Chino schools, anticipating a child in June. She had taught for four years and gave private music lessons after school hours.[10] She says she is looking forward to more free time and hopes to be able to continue her music classes at home after her child has arrived.

In reply to the "Present Status" question, another girl wrote, "I am married, have a year old child, and do not work at the present. (As if it wasn't work to keep up with a year old child, but I know what you mean.)" She has been with the Padua Theatre group, and completed her college education with very little financial assistance from home. She remarked that she had worked since she was fifteen years of age, and had incurred many debts in order to finish her studies, but these she was happily able to repay the first year, during which she was employed as a teacher in the high school at Norwalk, California. She is a graduate of Chaffey Junior College, Pomona College, and Claremont College, and has taught three years in the California schools.

---

[10]It is the policy of most of the local communities to employ Mexican teachers for Mexican children, when they are available.

45

Indirectly it was learned that one of the girls who graduated in June 1941, had been married to an American boy and was living in West Riverside. As none of her friends knew exactly where she could be found, and her family had moved, leaving no forwarding address, actual contact with her could not be made. It was said, however, that she was skillful with her needle, and had always intended to become a dressmaker. Her friends believed that this might be her occupation at the present time.

One girl completed her education at Santa Barbara State College, specializing in the teaching of small children. She teaches Mexican folk music and dancing to the other pupils in her school as well, often giving programs for other schools and organizations. It is her opinion that, through her ability to understand the little Mexican children in her room, she is able to help them translate their ideas into more facile English, and that since they know that she, too, is a Mexican, her example encourages them to learn.

Another girl has become a teacher in the Jordan High School in Los Angeles. Languages have held her dominating interest, and she now has classes in French, Spanish and English, having also taught German. She is a graduate of the University of Southern California at Los Angeles, and obtained her Master of Arts degree there in an additional year. She states that at one time she had decided to become a physician, taking all her junior college work to that end, but that her interest in languages became the determining factor in her life, and she is happy in the choice she made.

Of the girls who took commercial courses at Chaffey, one is at present secretary to the manager at Padua Hills. She was most enthusiastic about her position, as it permitted her to enter into a pleasant atmosphere, where the best in Mexican folklore is exemplified, and where she is in daily contact with congenial Mexican people, as well as with American people who are interested in the Mexican.

Another of these girls has been office manager of a lumber company in Albuquerque, New Mexico, since her graduation from Chaffey Junior College six years ago. She is married to an American, and together they have established a "better than average home." She is in charge of the office, filling also the position of bookkeeper and telephone operator.

Two of the girls from this field are temporarily unemployed, but both have had stenographic experience since their graduation. One states that she was offered a place as government stenographer, but that it entailed leaving her family for a long time--a condition which did not meet with their approval. She has registered with many employment agencies in Los Angeles, and feels sure that she will soon have the kind of situation she wants. She adds, "I have had several opportunities, but I want to make the most salary I can. Since I have so much experience back of me, I should be able to make more than a beginner, even if I am a Mexican."

The other girl who is looking for employment has had a series of illnesses that have limited her opportunities. She has become so discouraged that she is almost ready to end her search for work. She says that when she does secure a good position, some illness overtakes her and she is forced to resign. She is engaged to be married but the young man has just been called into the army, so her "bad luck" seems to pursue her. She hopes to move to Los Angeles as soon as she recovers from her present disability, so that she may have better medical treatment and, at the same time, a wider selection of positions from which to choose.

After completing high school, another of the girls attended an Ontario beauty college where she obtained her license to become a beauty operator. She has been continuously employed in this work, either in Pomona or Ontario, since her graduation. She states that this field is opening to Mexican girls, particularly in the Chaffey district, and is becoming an incentive to an increasing number of Mexican girls to complete their high school education, as that is a required qualification.

One girl has made an opening for herself out of the misfortune of war. She went immediately upon word of the evacuation of the Japanese to the San Fernando district to take over a contract held by Japanese for the hiring of labor to cut asparagus. She was successful in assembling her crews, and expects to be engaged there until October. At that time she will return to the position she has held since her graduation, with a department store in Pomona. Her new occupation is a far cry from her usual one, but she says that she has always wanted to "be the boss," and when she heard of the big opportunity she was glad to try it.

Another girl in the group has had no position since she graduated a year ago. Her mother became ill soon after that event, and upon her fell the task of supervising the rather large family still at home. She does not consider this too much

47

of a burden, as her brothers and sisters help her, and the housework gives her an opportunity to put into practice what she learned in the home-making class at Chaffey.

The last of the girls in the group is employed at present as sales clerk in a dress shop in Los Angeles, and is at the same time taking a nurses' preparatory course in night school. All of these endeavors are soon to end, however, as she expects to be married in the near future.

The foregoing records seem to establish the fact that these unusual Mexicans have in almost every instance attempted to use their education to good advantage. They have not always succeeded, but one must bear in mind that the year in which this study was made was, on account of the war, by no means an average year. Whether, in more normal times, these boys and girls could have found satisfactory positions must remain an open question, although almost everyone concerned said that work of some kind had always been obtainable. The opportunity afforded by the openings for young men in the army and the defense plants is made to order for advancing the position of the Mexican. The young people feel very conscious of their responsibility and are very desirous of "doing their part" to help the country in its time of need, hoping, at the same time, to help raise the status of the Mexican people in the eyes of the American public.

F.   Home and Community Status

The young people who have established homes of their own have adopted American furnishings, with only an occasional piece of typically Mexican pottery, picture, serape, or linen to accent the decoration. Some of the homes had hand-drawn pictures by Mexican artists, and one informant spoke of owning a complete set of Mexican dinner pottery and hand-blown glass ware. However, the homes visited showed no more of Mexican motif than almost any home in southern California. The influence of color from the Mexican folk art is apparent in most of the homes in this section. Except for the fact that most of the homes were located in the Mexican communities, and resembled them externally, the equipment was typically American and showed the ready assimilation of American home customs.

The young people living in the homes of their parents were surrounded with more of the typically Mexican equipment in that the furniture, in most instances, was covered with bright serapes, the pictures were of a more religious nature, the

48

floor coverings were apt to be linoleum, and the window curtains of lace or net rather than draped, or covered by Venetian blinds.

In the case of the young man who has assumed the support of his family, the home was a compromise between the things that pleased him and the furnishings of his mother's choosing. He said that he had chosen the rug, the drapes and a new divan, so that his home would be more "American" looking. This boy was, in fact, the "head" of the family and felt responsible for the welfare of his younger brother and sister, who are attending Chaffey.

The young women who have married and are classed as "housewives" are attempting to bring into their homes the American customs they have been taught in the home-making classes. One girl said that she had just completed recovering an over-stuffed chair, and that she had learned the "trick" in school. Most of the girls make their own clothes. They seemed as up-to-the-minute as any other group. Almost every home had a sewing machine, although it was seldom electric.

The children were dressed neatly and in modern manner, the mothers having made their clothes in most cases. In one family the children were being taught only English, so that it would be their "mother tongue." The parents planned to send the children to Mexico when they were six or seven years old, to live with the mother's people and learn Spanish from them. The parents felt that any vestige of foreign accent was a handicap to their children in this country. Other parents expressed the hope that they might put their children in a school attended by both Mexican and American children, so that they might learn the American manner of doing things, at the most impressionable time of their lives. Most of the communities in this study have separate schools for Mexican children until they reach the junior high and secondary schools.

On this subject a boy in the army wrote:

> "You know that the Mexican children, especially in Upland, are sent to schools, dilapidated shacks, separated from the American children. I think that is very wrong. I went through that school and I know how I felt. In the first place, it gave me the feeling of inferiority which I found hard to overcome. In the second place, it forms dislike, distrust, and even hatred of the American children. In the third place the Mexican children do not get to associate with the American children and pick up their customs, habits, and vice versa. This I think is serious. I think one of the basic reasons for segregation is the fact that some of the Mexican people are not neat (sic).

But it is like every other race. We have all kinds, clean, dirty, neat and not neat. Don't you think that a not neat Mexican child would tend to make himself neater and cleaner and try to match himself with the other children around him? And wouldn't he learn to like and respect his class and playmates? They would grow up together from primary school, perhaps through high school and university, and grow to understand each other's customs, habits and language."

This type of comment is not an isolated one. In almost every case the young people felt that the formative years that they had passed in separate schools were in part responsible for the lack of understanding between the groups. The athletic contests that take place between the "Mexican" schools and the "American" schools become almost international competitions for the honor of the race. The racial feeling engendered by this type of meeting is fuel to the fire of misunderstanding and prejudice. This fact suggests the desirability of making school experience the means of achieving the accommodation of the two groups, rather than a cause for conflict.

The dynamic effect of the school experience in this process is suggested by the fact that in every instance the young people were bringing the bits of American culture taught them into their homes. There seemed to be a conscious desire to take the best that our culture offered, but not to the exclusion of Mexican culture. It was commonly felt that there was much to be gained from retention of their native culture. The blending of the two cultures is the ultimate hope of each. Yet at present, in a desire to accord those things labeled "Mexican" a place with the ranking arts of the world (as opera is labeled "Italian" and progress in mechanical arts labeled "American"), the Mexican takes a more than expected interest in the arts and welfare of the ancestral country. They say, "Since I am called a Mexican, regardless of my birthright, then I want to be proud of the crafts that stem from Mexico."

The parents and families of these unusual Mexicans are proud of the accomplishments of their children. The opportunity for an education had been denied most of them, and for this reason education had become a symbol of the "better things of life." Education, per se, stood for all of the opportunities that they desired for their children: the security of a living wage, the finer comforts, a chance for equality with other groups. To such an extent has this conception been built up, that the young people complain that their parents are disappointed in their positions upon graduation from high school, feeling that a high school diploma should entitle them to professional standing. The status of a college graduate has been mistakenly given the high school graduate. This misunderstanding is widespread, and the young people who do manage to finish high school are put under a tremendous pressure by the misconception of the whole community as to the worth of their education. When the graduates attempt to explain that to become a teacher requires from four to five years more of study beyond high school, their parents and friends become discouraged for them and urge them to use what training they have, without attempting more. Or they suspect the young people of producing an alibi in an endeavor to avoid working. The parent who understands the value of a professional education urges his children to continue through school.[11] Occasionally it is the young person himself who works on toward the goal of a college degree; as in the case of the young man who is working his way through the University of California at the present time. It is in truth the acid test for ambition, and those Mexicans who succeed in completing college deserve all the recognition accorded them.

Educational Standing of the Study Group

Total Number	37
High School, Number Completing	37
Junior College, Number Attending or Completing	18
College, Number Attending or Completing	6
Master of Arts Degree	2

These young people exert a tremendous influence in their homes and communities. They are the "elite." The serious minded members of the Mexican group recognize their perseverance. They become the leaders in the activities of their communities, and are called upon to furnish programs, direct group thought, and represent the

---

[11]That the families within this study are more than usually conscious of the value of education is borne out by the number of brothers and sisters who attended high school and college.

	Total	Brothers	Sisters
High School	51	30	21
Junior College and College	11	3	8
Master of Arts Degree	2	1	1

Mexican group in intercommunity life. The less serious minded, as might be expected, look upon them as being "different," and suspect them of "putting on airs." The young people confess that this small minority of their own people causes them more embarrassment than the few Americans who discriminate against them. They are helpless before the sarcasm of this minority, and can use as their only weapon the evident fact of superior positions in the working world, and the possession of more of the commodities which spell success.

This attitude of cynical antagonism acts as a goad to the ambitions of the group. One boy, according to his own statement, moved into Los Angeles, after a summer spent in fruitless search for a good job near his home, to escape the constant reminder of some of the Mexicans in his community that he was a "big shot," and where was the "white collar job." He says that he would have starved rather than go out in the fields with former classmates who had quit school to work. "You have to get a better job," he adds, "so that the other parents will let their children go on to school. Some of them just sit around and wait for us to holler 'Uncle,' so they can say that our education didn't do us any good. I went into Los Angeles to find a decent job, and I didn't come home until I found one. I didn't want my mother and father to have to listen to some of the neighbors talk about me."

Almost all of the young people suffered some of this criticism. One girl tells of being injured just the day before she was to have entered upon a position as court interpreter in Riverside, and of how embarrassed she was to hear her mother explain, over and over, in the months she spent recuperating, that she really had had an opportunity to be "somebody." "As if," she comments, "I had to have an excuse for being at home." Another girl says that her family made it a point to let the neighbors know that she had passed a civil service examination, but that they would not let her accept the position since it meant that she would have to move to Washington, D.C. "It is true," she adds, "but I don't care what the neighbors say. We pay our bills and get along, and I'll get a better position somewhere closer home."

The activities of some of the members of the group under study seem pertinent to the position which they hold in their communities. The attitude of a few of their countrymen tends to turn the group in upon itself, or limits their influence to the more serious minded members of their communities, as has been pointed out.

This segment, however, encompasses the great majority of the Mexicans in the district. Therefore, the activities of the unusual Mexican under discussion, form a pattern of conduct for many of their countrymen and more especially for the younger children in the homes or grammar schools who have reached the "hero worship" stage in their lives. That the pattern for imitation is set by such a group is one of the encouraging aspects of the process of assimilation in America.

Among leadership activities are the baseball clubs many of the boys in the study have formed for younger boys. One informant relates that he was able to get the use of a vacant lot in his neighborhood, and to organize the young boys into teams which practiced after school hours, with his coaching, until he felt that they were able to carry on for themselves. He says that they occasionally come to him for decisions, although the organization took place some months ago. He believes that the whole community has benefited by the formation of the club, since busy young boys are not often bad young boys. Other boys tell of similar experiences in which football or basketball were the "modus operandi," but all agree that the "small fry" were more than grateful for the recognition given them, and repaid the older boys with blind devotion, listening to advice that was wasted on them by their parents.

Perhaps the most significant movement is the newly organized junior college boys' club called "Los Colegentes Mexicanos," which had its inception among the boys still attending Chaffey Junior College. Its purpose is to encourage Mexican boys to continue through junior college, and it aims at establishing a scholarship fund which could be used by members to continue their education. The boys hope to attract the attention of service clubs and other organizations which may see the desirability of such a plan. Six of the boys in this study are members and are increasingly enthusiastic about their new venture.

The Mexican Teachers Organization has been established within the last few years, bringing together the Mexican teachers in the public schools, so that they may pool their problems and work out solutions together. Two of the teachers in this study are members and feel that it is of great benefit to the Mexican people as a whole, since one of the aims of the organization is to encourage Mexican young people in the secondary schools to prepare themselves for teaching positions.

Perhaps the most inspiring of the Mexican groups is the general conference of all of the Mexican clubs throughout the state, which join in the spring of each year to consider the outstanding problems of this minority group. Prominent men of both Mexican and "Anglo-American" extraction appear before these club leaders and attempt to reach with them working solutions that will be of direct benefit to their own people. It is encouraging to note that at the conference held at Pacific Palisades, April 25 and 26, 1942, the subjects discussed covered: Discrimination against Mexican workers in defense plants; the undesirability of importing farm labor from Mexico (until assured by the United States Department of Labor that no other source of supply was available); the place of the Mexican-American in the war effort; the necessity for increasing the clubs of high-purposed young people to combat a new element rising in the "Pachuca"[12] gangs in the larger cities; the desirability of the development of leadership among the high school boys to prepare them to take the places of the older boys called into service, and also the development of girls' clubs as rapidly as possible to fill the same need.

---

[12]The "Pachuca" is described, by the young people who brought the problem before the conference, as a boy or girl of Mexican parentage who dresses in the extreme style characterized on the part of the boy by high-waisted, tight-legged trousers, long hair and side-burns, while the girl wears short, tight skirts, and blouses usually embroidered with a black cross. In many cases they carry knives which they seem not only willing but anxious to use. They affect this type of clothing as a badge or "regalia" in an attempt further to dissociate themselves from other Mexican boys and girls. For the most part, they represent an undesirable element, and they have formed bands for the express purpose of breaking up meetings, dances, and other forms of diversion.

The young people in this study are of the opinion that the indirect reason for the formation of such gangs is to offset the strides toward "Americanism" made by the serious minded. This movement has been gathering much momentum in the last few years, and has shown such progress that easily led members of many Mexican communities have taken this means of showing their antagonism toward the values propounded by the more progressive elements. The gravity of the problem is not immediately apparent in the Chaffey district, as the organized gangs seem to be confined to the Los Angeles area, but the danger lies in the unknowing imitation of many of the young people in our section. There are girls and boys in our own communities who are dressed in much the same fashion, and who are pitied for their lack of taste rather than told of the implication of their mode of dress. The young leaders of thought among the Mexicans have been made aware of the possible problem confronting them, and will prepare to take steps to meet it. The conference suggested that the approach should be made from the psychological angle, as a direct method might serve only to drive these groups closer together in organized form. The unfortunate fact that the vandalism of these few can do more to injure the reputation of the Mexican in our country than all the good work combined can offset, is not lost on the young people of serious intent.

(These would of course be limited by the restrictions imposed by the fathers' invincible desire to control the movements of their daughters.)

The conference passed two resolutions. The first, addressed to the President of the United States, included the assurance of the group of their whole-hearted agreement with the principles propounded in the "Atlantic Charter," and of their desire to be in all ways of assistance to this country in its hour of need. The other resolution was addressed to the Secretary of Agriculture, requesting him not to consider the importation of Mexican labor until all other possible sources had been exhausted.

Three of the boys included in this study attended the conference as delegates from "Los Colegentes Mexicanos," the newly formed college-boys' club. One of the study group was elected vice-president for the ensuing year, while another member of the club was elected president. This action assures the Chaffey district of leaders in the youth movement for several years.

CHAFFEY HIGH SCHOOL GRADUATES

Rodolfo Sanchez	1932	Construction work, carpenter
Joe Trujillo	1933	Ranch manager
Cruz Huerta (Hodges)	1934	Office manager, Lumber Co.
Esperanza Calleros	1936	Secretary (temporarily unemployed)
Aureliano Ruiz	1936	Store manager (grocery and meats)
Paul Ynastrosa	1936	Corporal, U.S. Army Air Corps
Manuel Guerrero	1937	Barber (defense work)
Pascual Castro	1938	Washer, Ontario laundry
Calistro Gomez	1938	Student Chaffey J.C. (aviation)
Florence Guttierez	1938	Contract employer of asparagus pickers
Raymond Santoyo	1938	Tractor mechanic (temporarily unemployed)
Henrietta Zamorano	1938	Beauty Operator
Isadore Romero	1939	Ranch work (tractor workers)
Guadalupe Vega	1939	Maintains family home
Henry Savala	1940	Salesman, May Company
Ramiro Gomez	1940	Student, Chaffey J.C.
Enrique Martinez	1940	Private, U.S. Army
Samuel Montoyo	1940	Welder, Consolidated Aircraft Co.
Petra Romero	1940	Student, Chaffey J.C.
Rafael Castro	1941	Student, Chaffey J.C. (aviation)
Johnny Martinez	1941	Student, Chaffey J.C.
Victoria Razo (Quesado)	1941	Housewife
Manuel Rodriguez	1941	Lemon picker
Jesus Sandoval	1941	Student, Chaffey J.C.
David Olivarez	1941	Lemon picker

CHAFFEY JUNIOR COLLEGE GRADUATES

Alicia Espinosa (Cortez)	1932	Housewife (teacher)
Mary Garcia	1932	Teacher, Secondary School, Los Angeles
Manuela Huerta	1932	Housewife (teacher)
Emma Lopez	1932	Teacher
Paul Leos*	1936	Staff Sergeant, Interceptor Command
Ernest Asebedo*	1938	Private, U.S. Army
Antonio de Valles*	1938	Student, University of California
Porfidia Lopez	1939	Secretary
Alicia Marquez	1940	Secretary (unemployed)
Virginia Garcia	1941	Sales clerk in dress shop

High School	30
Junior College	12
Total	42
Duplicates	3
Total Interviewed	37

---

* Also completed Chaffey High School.

CHAPTER IV

TENTATIVE CONCLUSIONS

The evidence presented in the foregoing chapters suggests that the unusual Mexican tends to be much like other Mexicans in the following respects.

A. Cultural Backgrounds

The young people in the study were the accepted Mexican type. Their coloring was little different from the average of any group of Mexicans, although it is true that in many families some of the children are lighter than the others. It is commonly said in describing a brother or sister, "He is much lighter than I," or "She is much darker than I am." Some of the families interviewed were generally lighter in complexion than others, while some were as dark as any of the Mexicans in the district. There was no marked divergence from the usual Mexican, in respect to color, among the members of this unusual group.

Their families migrated to the United States at about the same time as the general Mexican migration took place. The years from 1900 to 1926 cover the entry of the group into this country. With the exception of one father, who had been born here and had made a place for himself, the parents of the group came empty-handed. They came to find work, and to escape the uncertainty of making a living in a country torn by revolution. The informants emphasized the fact that there were no lofty reasons for the transference of their families to the United States.

The fathers had engaged in much the same kinds of work in Mexico as had the other Mexican migrants, with two exc eptions. They were, for the most part, laborers on ranches, craftsmen or tradesmen. They came from the great plateau region of Mexico, from the small villages that sleep in the yesterdays of civiliza-tion. They were steeped in the lore of their folk ways, and geared to a life in which there is always time for enjoying the day as it comes.

Some of the parents have joined groups that have been formed in this country through the office of the Mexican consul, namely, La Commision Honorifica and La Aliansa Hispan-America. These societies are bulwarks against the inundating tide of American culture. They celebrate El Cinco de Mayo and El Dies-y-sies de Setembre, national Mexican holidays, and these groups are as much a part of the

Mexican pattern in this country as the newest migrant from Mexico. The old ways have been remembered and the parents wish their children to remember them. It is the natural desire of a people to be proud of their ancestry, and the Mexican is not understood unless his great pride in his own people is taken into account.

The parents in almost every instance speak only Spanish or very poor English. They explain that they had come to the United States after their "tongues were set." Many of them state that they have attended night classes in an attempt to learn English, but that the lack of formal education in Mexico was a great handicap in the acquiring of another language, since a few of them could not even read Spanish. Others said that they had had elementary schooling in Mexico and that they were, in some cases, able to learn to read English from the newspapers. The majority of them confessed, however, that they had not needed English badly enough to have been forced to learn it, for they lived among Mexicans, shopped in stores where Spanish was spoken, and used the knowledge of their children in any unusual circumstance.

Only a few of the parents had applied for citizenship papers. The excuse was much the same as above, but with the added reason that it did little good to have American citizenship without the right of equality. They point out that, by retaining their Mexican citizenship, they have the right of redress through the Mexican consular office. Since the rapprochement of the two governments under the stimuli of war this attitude seems to be diminishing, and an increasing number of parents are applying for citizenship papers. They say that since their sons are being called to defend this country, they have an incentive to become citizens.

B. Native Endowments

The unusual Mexican has not distinguished himself in school by outstanding grades. A check of the available grade records kept at Chaffey showed that the members of this group averaged "C" grade through high school. A check of other Mexican students, at present attending Chaffey or who had "dropped out," showed much the same grades. Some of the students received better marks in a particular subject, but tended to fall below average in other classes. As an example, the boy with the exceptional ability in art received "A" throughout his four year course in that subject, but did not receive as good marks in many of the other courses.

The graduates in the study said that they were not outstanding students. They mentioned other girls and boys who had surpassed them in grammar school and in high school, but remarked that many of this group did not continue their education because of economic necessity in the home, or a desire to marry, or to "drop out," as they had fulfilled the age requirement and had no wish to go on. It was their opinion that economic necessity was the greatest handicap the Mexican is obliged to face in obtaining an education. None of the families included in this study can "hand an education" to their children. In the majority of cases the young people are bearing their own expenses, in some instances backed by sacrifices on the part of the family.

The young people felt that their number could have been legion if intelligence or artistic ability were the key. They emphasized the fact that they were just about like other Mexicans, admitting that they were brighter than some with whom they had gone to school, but they were sure that intelligence was not the primary factor in the selection of their group.

C. Home Background

The exterior of the homes of the majority of the group is identical with the homes of other Mexicans in their community. There were eight homes classified as excellent which cannot be considered as typically Mexican. They are the California bungalow type which can be seen anywhere in southern California. The significant facts to be remembered, however, are that only two of the homes were not located in the Mexican districts, and that, in general, equally attractive homes were occupied by ordinary Mexicans.

The furnishings in some instances were superior to the furnishings in other homes but, again, the comparison is among the Mexicans themselves. Therefore it can be assumed that the standards set by the Mexican communities have not been surpassed by any of the families considered in this study.

The family structure is much the same. The numbers of children per family do not suggest that education was made easier by small families. The 6.05 children of the families studied is above the United States average by 4.25 children per family.[1] Yet the average for Mexican families for California is 5.8, showing that these families are above the average for their own group.

D. Employment of Father

The fathers of this unusual group were found to be engaged in much the same type of labor, as the great majority were employed in the fruit industries. The types of employment are listed as follows:

Total	37
Fruit Industries (picking, farming)	20
Dairy (proprietors)	2
Railroad Mechanic	2
Carpenter	2
Blacksmith	2
Cement Company (laborers)	2
Lumber Mill (laborer)	1
Water Company (laborer)	1
Stockyard Proprietor	1
Paymaster Sugar Beet Co.	1
Fertilizer Company (laborer)	1
Restaurant and Bar (proprietor)	1
Minister	1

It is to be seen that these men are in jobs that require physical labor, for the most part. Only two of the men hold so-called "white-collar" positions.

In spite of the factors enumerated above, which showed the background of the unusual Mexican to be that common to his countrymen, the facts tend to identify him as a transitional cultural type, because in every instance he accepts and is marked by the typical patterns of the assimilating group. Evidence of the acculturation of this group is to be found in the following tendencies toward adjustment.

His Home

Although, as has been mentioned, the exterior of the homes of the group encompassed in this study, and the furnishings as well, are much like those of other Mexican families of like income, the "atmosphere" of the home of our unusual Mexican

---

[1] In 1940 there were in the United States 34,861, 625 families with an average of 3.8 persons per family, or 1.8 children. Source: 15th Census of the U.S., 1940.

is definitely American. That is, the arrangement of the furniture, the color schemes, the kinds of pictures or prints on the walls, the use of certain articles of furniture (spinet pianos, Winchester desks, studio couches, light woodwork, modern kitchen equipment) have a decided American flavor. Although all of these articles were not present in any one home, the presence of any one of them, or combination of them, indicated a long step from the typical home of the Mexican immigrant. The young couples who had established homes of their own were selecting the more modern "Swedish," or "chrome" type of furnishings, in every instance well blended with some treasured Mexican art piece. There were few homes where an American housewife would have felt out of her element. The desire to make the home like American homes was present, regardless of ability to purchase American furniture.

His Patterns of Family Life

The homes of the married couples with children were the ones in which the patterns were more clearly defined. These young people were rearing their children in a manner far different from the methods used with themselves by their own parents. One young mother commented that her mother thought she was too concerned with the health of her child, because she took her baby to the "Well Baby Clinics" held in Ontario each month. The shots for diphtheria and whooping cough had been administered over the protest of the grandmother, although she had not objected to the vaccination for smallpox. Another young mother confided that her own mother had felt she was pampering herself when she insisted that her child was to be born in a hospital. She added triumphantly, "I stayed ten days like you are supposed to, and I didn't get up at home until the doctor said I should."

One of the girls said that the neighbors gave advice to her about the rearing of children that she knew was incorrect, if not injurious. She was in a dilemma until she hit upon the happy plan of doing what she knew was best, and agreeing at the same time to follow the well meant advice. The persistence of the herbal folk lore in America is vouched for by the many persons in the Mexican communities who practice a rather "left-handed" form of pharmacy. Some of the young girls stated that the only medicines in their homes, as children, were different kinds of dried leaves and ointments made by the "medicine women" in their communities.

Of the young people who are still in the family homes, it can be said that their lives are a compromise with the old ways. The parents continue many of the customs of Mexico that do not interest or please the young people. Yet these younger members of the family say that their parents are willing to adopt American patterns when shown their value. The most persistent carry-over is the protection accorded young girls. This seems to be the most obstinate barrier between the old ways and the new. The boys mentioned the fact that the pitied their sisters, since they had to be engaged before the parents permitted them to go about freely. This custom is slowly breaking down, however, as the younger members of the group admitted that older brothers and sisters had "worked on the mothers and fathers so much about it" that they were being accorded more liberty.

The mothers in the group did not wear the reboso; not once was that head covering in evidence. The girls and boys say that they are embarrassed by their mothers when they appear on the streets with a reboso, or head shawl. Perhaps this explains the breaking away from the custom.

His Attitude Toward Education

There is no question as to the positive attitude toward education held by these young people. They have placed a premium on it. Yet they are not blind to the fact that education in itself is not the greatest problem; it is merely a tool which enables them to carve out a place for themselves in a passive society. One young man said, "I have never been able to use any of the courses I took in high school, in a practical way. But I am thankful every day of my life that I have had them. When my neighbors are worried about the war, I get out my history books and read about other wars, and find peace in the knowledge that all things have ended in the past, and will in the future. I can remember some of the poetry that I had in English, and it makes the days more beautiful to know how to say their beauty. I have never worked a geometry problem since the last day of my course, but I know that I could if I had to, and knowing that makes me sure of myself in other ways. No, I don't regret a day I spent in school; they were the happiest of my life. Believe me, my children are going to have all the education they want."

Attitudes Toward Religion

The drift from strict Catholicism among this group indicates a leavening effect of the Protestant movement in the United States. The large number of the group who professed allegiance to one or another of the forms of Protestantism in this country, had made the change from Catholicism since the migration of the family. The breaking away from the regime of the Catholic church, although not complete, seems to be increasing. The number of young people who classed themselves as "good" Catholics was small in comparison to the number who confessed that they were only "fair" or "poor" Catholics. It is not the intention of this study to interpret this as a "good" or "bad" sign, but to point out that in the assimilation of religious patterns, as well as other cultural patterns, the group seems to be following the general trend of American life.

His Employment is More Like Typical American Employment

As has been noted, the unusual Mexican is employed in more different types of positions than his father and less fortunate countrymen. A drift toward semi-skilled, skilled and professional activities seems to be generally true of this group. The tendency to complete junior college, and to continue collegiate education, opens to it the field of the professions. Teaching is the wedge for a majority of college trained Mexicans. The opportunities offered in the armed services for the boys in the group is unlimited. There they will be on equal footing with the native white population. The editor of "Mexican Voice," a publication of the Youth Conference, says:

> "When we answered 'yes' on 'war has some benefits' we were thinking of our Mexican-American youth. We were thinking of the future and how the Americans of other descents would look upon the Mexican-American. We also looked at the background of the average Mexican-American in the service. Usually he came from 'Mexican town' where he attended 'Mexican school.' Not until high school did he associate with Americans of other racial and social backgrounds. At present he is thrown into constant contact with all backgrounds. He is now on an equal basis with lawyer Burn's pampered son. Or perchance he and Joe Gordon of the Toonerville Gordons now share food and assignments. In their home town Joe Gordon wouldn't have looked twice at our Mexican-American. The services have helped our Mexican-American. It has dressed all alike and given opportunities for advancement on merit and work. It has given many of our shy, inferior feeling Americans of Mexican descent a chance to learn

63

something, a chance to fit into the scheme of things, a chance to belong. The war in this respect is doing what we in our Mexican-American movement had planned to do in one generation."[2]

Patriotism, Social and Civic Responsibilities

Finally, the attitudes of the unusual Mexican, as expressed in the sentiments of patriotism, social and civic responsibilities, tend to identify him as an integral part of this country. Perhaps the unusual times in which we live are in part responsible for the display of the qualities of the members of this group. The "pacifist era" in which most of them were raised was not conducive to an outward demonstration of patriotism. When children are lined up each morning and told to salute the flag, it is not uncommon for the young ones to end the recitation with a rousing iteration, "We are Mexicans!" This is not done in a spirit of defiance, but in recognition of the obvious place accorded them by the majority of Americans.

Now, when it is again patriotic to show one's love of country, the young Mexican-Americans are joining the services and entering into the "all-out defense" of this country with spirit. In an article headed "Nosotros," Manuel de la Raza says:

> "In our local draft board there was a high rate of volunteers of Americans of Mexican descent. What this proves we cannot venture to guess. But ... it is heartening because they, relatively, have less to fight for than the fellows 'north of the railroad tracks.' These fellows, for the most part, had never felt American. They had never been given the chance. At home their parents had derided 'Americans.' Any sign of gruffness, of coldness, of unpoliteness, and of excessive noise was considered 'American' to them. In the schools, by attending 'their own,' they couldn't feel American. In the municipal plunge a day was reserved for the 'Mexicans.' In the theatre the right side was for 'them.' Certain restaurants would not cater to 'Mexicans.' Yet ... somehow these fellows enlisted, joined the ranks, and shouldered the responsibility as theirs. The war has served to unite the majority and minority groups in our home towns. It has shown those 'across the tracks' that we all share the same problems. It has shown what the Mexican-American will do, what responsibility he will take, and what leadership qualities he will demonstrate. After this stuggle the status of the Mexican-American will be different."[3]

---

[2]Manuel de la Raza, "Nosotras," Mexican Voice, Vol. I: 6 April 1942.

[3]Loc. cit.

In this eloquent appeal to fair-mindedness speak the new leaders of America, regardless of their extraction. It is in the common understanding of the problems that confront us that the nation finds its strength. From across the tracks, from the shanty towns, from the 'Mexican towns,' come the girls and boys in this study. That they have demonstrated their willingness to go more than half way in the acceptance of American standards is seen in their determination to raise themselves above the level of their compatriots. But this struggle has never had a personal motive; it is not an expression of typical "rugged individualism"; it has held always something of the missionary spirit, the desire to rise, but in rising to carry with them the less ambitious, the less fortunate.

The Unusual Mexican is Unusual in only one aspect: he has graduated from high school or junior college. This is the postulate with which we began. But in the adherence to American patterns, in the acceptance of our standard of educational fitness, these young people have shown their willingness to conform, to assimilate. They have taken from this country the priceless gift of an education freely offered to all, and in return they give to this country the leaders of tomorrow, the brown-skinned "man of the future," who believes in the words of the great Ezequiel Padilla: "Democracy is a sacred cause." That the United States will be stronger for that belief and for those who follow it is borne out by the fact that these young people are assimilating the major elements of the American cultural pattern, and are thereby rendering more readily assimilable in the American community their fellow countrymen.

BIBLIOGRAPHY

Aikman, Duncan, The All-American Front. New York: Doubleday, Doran and Company, 1941. 344 pp.

Bancroft, Hubert Howe, History of Mexico. San Francisco: The History Company, 1886. Vols. 9-14. 4,673 pp.

Beals, Carlton, Mexico--An Interpretation. New York: B. W. Huebsch, Inc., 1923. 280 pp.

_____, Mexican Maze, J. B. Lippincott Company, Philadelphia: 1931. 369 pp.

Bogardus, Emory S., The Mexican in the United States. Los Angeles: University of Southern California Press, 1934. 126 pp.

_____, Immigration and Race Attitudes. New York: D. C. Heath and Company, 1928. 268 pp.

_____, Contemporary Sociology, Los Angeles: University of Southern California Press, 1932. 483 pp.

Brenner, Anita, Idols Behind Altars. New York: Payson and Clark, 1929. 259 pp.

Case, A. B., Thirty Years with the Mexicans. New York: Fleming Revell Company, 1917. 285 pp.

Chase, Stuart, A Study of Two Americas. New York: The MacMillan Company, 1931. 338 pp.

Creel, George, The People Next Door. New York: The John Day Company, 1926. 418 pp.

Dillon, E. J., Mexico on the Verge. New York: George H. Doran Company, 1921. 296 pp.

Ellwood, Charles A., and Howard Jensen, Methods in Sociology. Durham: Duke University Press, 1933. 214 pp.

Eubank, Earle E., The Concepts of Sociology. New York: D. C. Heath and Company, 1932. 570 pp.

Ferguson, Erna, Fiesta in Mexico. New York: A. A. Knopf, 1934. 267 pp.

Gamio, Manuel, Mexican Immigration to the United States. Chicago: University of Chicago Press, 1930. 262 pp.

Garner, Bess, Mexico: Notes in the Margin. Boston: Houghton Mifflin Company, 1937. 163 pp.

Gruening, Ernest, Mexico and its Heritage. New York: The Century Company, 1928. 728 pp.

Guttierez de Lara, Lazaro, The Mexican People, Their Struggle for Freedom. New York: Doubleday, Page and Company, 1924. 360 pp.

Hanna, Phil Townsend, Mexico in the Machine Age. Los Angeles: Alpha Delta Iota Press, 1832. 33 pp.

Herring, Hubert C., editor, The Genius of Mexico. New York: The Committee on Cultural Relations with Latin America, 1931. 334 pp.

Lasker, Bruno, Race Attitudes in Children. New York: Henry Holt and Company, 1929. 394 pp.

Lindeman, Edward C., Social Discovery. New York: Longmans-Green, 1925. 375 pp.

Lummis, Charles, The Awakening of a Nation. New York: Harper and Brothers, 1898. 179 pp.

McConnell, Burt, Mexico at the Bar of Public Opinion. New York: Mail and Express Publishing Company, 1939. 320 pp.

McLean, Robert N., That Mexican. New York: Fleming H. Revell Company, 1928. 184 pp.

Miller, Max, Mexico Around Me. New York: Reynal and Hitchcock, 1937. 305 pp.

Moats, Leone, Thunder in Their Veins. New York: The Century Company, 1932. 273 pp.

O'Brien, Robert, Mexicans and Crime in Southern California. Claremont: Lawson Roberts Publishing Company, 1927. 6 pp.

O'Saughnessy, Edith A., A Diplomat's Wife in Mexico. New York: Harper and Brothers, 1916. 335 pp.

_____, Diplomatic Days. New York: Harper and Brothers, 1917. 337 pp.

Parsons, Elsie Clews, Mitla: Town of Souls. Chicago: University of Chicago Press, 1936. 590 pp.

Plenn, J. H., Mexico Marches. New York: The Bobbs-Merrill Company, 1939. 386 pp.

Prescott, Wm. H., History of the Conquest of Mexico. New York: Harper and Brothers, 1834. 3 Volumes, 1,465 pp.

Priestly, Herbert Ingram, The Mexican Nation, A History. New York: The MacMillan Company, 1930. 507 pp.

Redfield, Robert, Tepoztlan, A Mexican Village. Chicago: University of Chicago Press, 1930. 247 pp.

Roa, Fernando Gonzales, The Mexican People and Their Detractors. New York: The Latin-American News Association, 1916. 92 pp.

Ross, Edward Alsworth, The Social Revolution in Mexico. New York: The Century Company, 1923. 176 pp.

Saenz, Moises and H. I. Priestly, Some Mexican Problems. Chicago: University of Chicago Press, 1926. 174 pp.

Spence, Lewis, Mexico of the Mexicans. New York: Charles Scribner's Sons, 1918. 232 pp.

Story, Russell M., Mexico. Claremont: Intra-American Institute, 1929. 104 pp.

Steinbeck, John, The Forgotten Village. New York: The Viking Press, 1941. 143 pp.

Tannenbaum, Frank, Peace by Revolution. New York: Columbia University Press, 1933. 316 pp.

Thomas, Wm. I., and Florian Znaniecki, The Polish Peasant in Europe and America. Chicago: University of Chicago Press, 1931. 315 pp.

Thompson, C. A., The Man From Next Door. New York: The Century Company, 1926. 234 pp.

Thompson, Wallace, The People of Mexico. New York: Harper and Brothers, 1921. 427 pp.

Trowbridge, E. D., Mexico, Today and Tomorrow. New York: The MacMillan Company, 1919. 282 pp.

Vasconcelos, Jose, and Manuel Gamio, Aspects of Mexican Civilization. Chicago: University of Chicago Press, 1926. 193 pp.

Walling, Wm. English, The Mexican Question. New York: Robins Press, 1927. 205 pp.

Watson, Goodwin, Education and Social Welfare in Mexico. New York: The Council for Pan-American Democracy, 1940. 131 pp.

Whitaker, Arthur P., editor, Mexico Today. Philadelphia: American Academy of Social Sciences, 1940. 252 pp.

Griffin, Charles C., Concerning Latin American Culture. New York: Columbia University Press, 1940. 234 pp.

GOVERNMENT DOCUMENTS

Republic of Mexico, Dept. of Labor, Policies of the Present Administration of Mexico. Mexico City: Government Printing Office, 1936. 70 pp.

Republic of Mexico, Dept. of Foregin Relations, The Mexican Government in the Presence of Social and Economic Problems. Mexico City: Ministry of Foreign Relations, 1936. 157 pp.

Republic of Mexico, Dept. of Foreign Relations, Ezequiel Padilla: Tres Discursos
    en Rio de Janeiro. Mexico City D.F.: Ministry of Foreign Relations.

Committee on Latin American Relations, The Seminar in Mexico: A Cooperative Study
    of Mexican Life and Culture. Mexico City D.F.: Committee on Latin American
    Relations, 1929. 137 pp.

State of California, Executive Dept., Governor C. C. Young's Mexican Fact-Finding
    Committee. San Francisco: California State Printing Office, 1930. 214 pp.

University of California, Heller Committee for Research in Social Economics, Cost
    of Living Studies V: How Mexicans Earn and Live. Berkeley: University of
    California Publications in Economics, Vol. 13: No. 1933. 114 pp.

U.S. Department of Agriculture, Rural Life Studies I, Culture of a Contemporary
    Rural Community. Washington, D.C.: Bureau of Agricultural Economics, 1941.
    72 pp.

NEWSPAPERS

El Espectador, Ontario, California, February 17, 1939
                                    February 24, 1939
                                    March 3, 1939
                                    October 6, 1939

The Daily Report, Ontario, California, March 4, 1939

UNPUBLISHED THESES

Anderson, Arthur, "The Study of the Ethnography of Mexico." Unpublished Master's
    thesis, Claremont College, Claremont, 1931. 102 pp.

Beard, E. Alice, "A Study of the Mexican Pupils in Fremont Junior High School."
    Unpublished Master's thesis, Claremont College, Claremont, 1941. 68 pp.

Drake, Rollin, "A Comparison of the Intelligence of Mexican Children." Unpublished
    Master's thesis, University of Southern California, Los Angeles, 1938.

Hanson, Stella E., "Mexican Laborers in the Southwest." Unpublished Master's
    thesis, Pomona College, Claremont, 1926. 239 pp.

Hayden, Jessie, "The La Habra Experiment." Unpublished Master's thesis, Claremont
    College, Claremont, 1934. 202 pp.

Hill, Merton E., "The Development of an Americanization Program at Chaffey Junior
    College." Unpublished Master's thesis, University of Southern California,
    Los Angeles, 1928. 235 pp.

Sauter, Mary, "Arbol Verde, A California Mexican Community." Unpublished Master's
thesis, Claremont College, Claremont, 1933. 214 pp.

Sauter, Mary, "San Diego Viejo." Unpublished dissertation, Claremont College,
Claremont, 1939. 394 pp.

MAGAZINES

Bogardus, Emory S., "Current Problems of Mexican Immigrants." Sociology and Social
Research, October 1940. pp. 166-174.

Kirk, William, "Cultural Conflicts in Mexican Life." Sociology and Social Research,
March-April 1931. pp. 352-364.

_____, "Current Social Movements in Mexico." Sociology and Social Research,
May-June, 1931. pp. 402-416.

Time, "Ezequiel Padilla: The American Man of the Future." April 6, 1942. pp. 29-32.

de la Raza, Manuel, "Nosotros." Mexican Voice, Spring, 1942. p. 8.

APPENDIX

CHAFFEY DISTRICT

Proportion of Mexican Graduates from High School and Junior College

	Number in High School Graduating Class		Number in Junior College Graduating Class	
	All	Mexicans [*]	All	Mexicans
1932	293	2	163	4
1933	300	1	206	0
1934	244	1	220	0
1935	299	0	192	0
1936	289	4	167	0
1937	279	1	209	0
1938	332	7	167	1
1939	355	2	202	3
1940	373	6	277	1
1941	370	6	258	3
Totals	3,134	30	2,071	12

---

[*] The names of Mexican graduates were taken from the graduation programs of the past ten years. There were no separate records kept of Mexican students, and consequently no means of obtaining the very pertinent data on numbers admitted to the original entering group. It would be informative to know the numbers of Mexican students in each of the entering groups, which would include the classes from 1928 to 1937.

MEXICAN HIGH SCHOOL GRADUATES 1932-1941

Name	Address	Year
Rodolpho Sanchez	Upland	1932
*Silvestre Santos	Alta Loma	1932
Joe Trujillo	Etiwanda	1933
Cruz Huerta	Ontario	1934
Paul Leos	Cucamonga	1936
Esperanza Calleros	Mira Loma	1936
Aureliano Ruiz	Ontario	1936
Paul Ynastrosa	Upland	1936
Manuel Guerrero	Ontario	1937
Ernest Asebedo	Upland	1938
Pascual Castro	Cucamonga	1938
Calistro Gomez	Upland	1938
Florence Guttierez	Upland	1938
Raymond Santoyo	Cucamonga	1938
Antonio de Valles	Ontario	1938
Henrietta Zamorano	Ontario	1938
Isadore Romero	Ontario	1939
Guadalupe Vega	Fontana	1939
Henry Savala	Fontana	1940
*Lucille Aguilar	Upland	1940
Ramiro Gomez	Claremont	1940
Enrique Martinez	Cucamonga	1940
Samuel Montoya	Fontana	1940
Petra Romero	Ontario	1940
Ralph Castro	Cucamonga	1941
Johnny Martinez	Cucamonga	1941
Victoria Razo	Ontario	1941
Manuel Rodriguez	Ontario	1941
Jesus Sandoval	Upland	1941
David Olivarez	Ontario	1941

High School Graduates 30
*
Unable to Locate 2

Total Graduates in Study 28

MEXICAN JUNIOR COLLEGE GRADUATES 1932-1941

Name	Address	Year
Alicia I. Espinoza	Chino	1932
Mary E. Garcia	Pomona	1932
Manuela Huerta	Ontario	1932
*Paul Leos	Cucamonga	1938
Fred Sanchez	Puente	1939
Dan Savala	Upland	1939
Porfidia Lopez	Chino	1939
Alicia Martinez	Chino	1940
*Ernest Asebedo	Upland	1941
Virginia Garcia	Chino	1941
*Anthony Valles	Cucamonga	1941

Junior College Graduates	12
High School Graduates	28
Total	40
*Graduates of Both Schools	3
Total in Study Group	37

THE CHAFFEY DISTRICT*

			Population by Township
1.	Ontario	School District	16,044
2.	Upland	School District	7,118
3.	Camp Baldy	School District	
4.	Etiwanda	School District	1,259
5.	Alta Loma	School District	
6.	Cucamonga	School District	5,483
7.	Guasti	School District	
8.	Mountain View	School District	
9.	Fontana	School District	4,115
10.	Chino	School District	7,362
(Covers an area of 222 square miles)			41,382

---

*U.S. Census, 1940.

A MENTAL SCHEDULE

Name   Born   Where?

Father

Mother

Siblings

Education

Church affiliation

When family came to U.S.

Where entered

Reasons for coming

Employment history and movement

Why family moved about

Why they settled here

Employment history in the community

Do they own their own home

Type of home

Accommodations

Luxuries

Citizenship status

Instances of racial conflict

Job history

Present status